PRE-TRIAL MOTIONS:

BEFORE THE

Infinity Court

Daniel A. Martens Yaverbaum

&

John Jay Physics

ISBN: 0-9985847-1-1
ISBN-s : 978-0-9985847-1-3

ACKNOWLEDGMENTS

DEPARTMENT OF SCIENCES,
JOHN JAY COLLEGE OF CRIMINAL JUSTICE,
THE CITY UNIVERSITY OF NEW YORK
NEW YORK, NY

TEACHERS COLLEGE,
COLUMBIA UNIVERSITY
NEW YORK, NY

SAINT ANN'S SCHOOL
BROOKLYN, NY

THE LAKEVILLE JOURNAL COMPANY, LLC
LAKEVILLE, CT

NOWHERE STUDIOS
BROOKLYN, NY

STARRY NIGHT PRO 7 SOFTWARE
SIMULATION CURRICULUM CORP.
MINNETONKA, MN

PIXTON COMICS INC.
PARKSVILLE, BRITISH COLUMBIA, CANADA

THE PUBLIC DOMAIN*
& ALL WHOLLY OWNED SUBSIDIARIES
INCLUDING BUT NOT RESTRICTED TO
THE INTERNET, ELECTROMAGNETIC SPACE & ASSOCIATES

MARTENS YAVERBAUM OSTERMAN MEYER FAMILIES
THEY THAN WHICH, NONE OTHER NEVER

---

*To the best of the author's knowledge, all images contained within are in the public domain or are the author's.

to M

who exercised infinite patience

USER's GUIDE
to

Infinity Court

Now... in BOARD GAME format...

'SMALL CLAIMS' v2.0!

For all our precious Travelin' Tots & Prime Movers!

Moms & Dads, premember!
Our precious little particles are radiating –
whether we're ready or not!
We can't be around to co-occupy every eigenstate they manifest.

You did your first job and kept them safe from the world;
now do your second job and teach them how to navigate its dangers & shadier zones—
but gently, at home, while having fun!

Premember! The earlier we can get our precious quarks and muons to take controlled risks
and build their infinity-immunities to reality's rougher regions
then it's just a lighter load for all!
Have courage! Show your the young 'uns what can happen between 'space' and 'time'
before they hear about it on the street!

Pick up and play:

'SMALL CLAIMS' (v2.0) (before the) *Infinity Court*

Available in Compact & EZ-Play
Version 2.0: Total game-play guaranteed for as few as 1.81 dimensions!

And now... game on!
Quickstart Guide on Next Page!

QUICKSTART

1. The hypothesis:

You are **HERE*** :

*stuck on the corner in a shady part of town:
stuck and lost in a rough neighborhood which swirls around
the intersection of 'space' and 'time'.

All the locals You are at a point known by the natives as

$$x o t o$$

2. The Challenge:

Get **THERE*** :

*to a point of infinite reward known by the natives as

$$point\ A$$

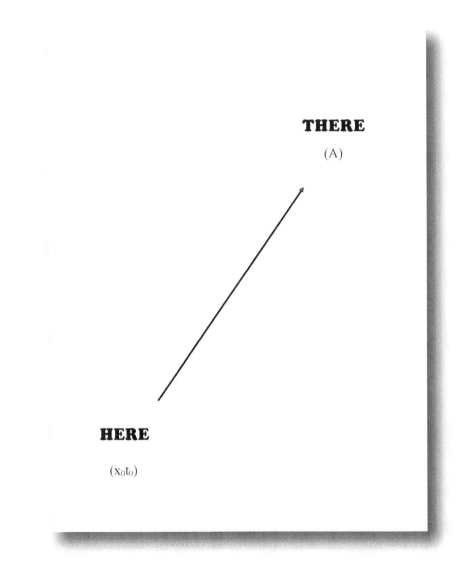

THERE

(A)

HERE

$(x_0 t_0)$

For tips on expert game play or help with the higher dimensions, please see the complete and comprehensive manual, aka 'the book':

Pre-Trial Motions Before the Infinity Court.

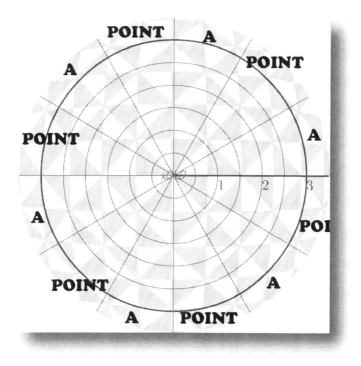

For a tip on how to endure or follow 'the book' (*Pre-Trial Motions...*),

Select your frame of Reference:

In a physics class?	Read at 2 knots
In law school or the like?	Read at 3 knots
On a dissertation committee?	Read at 5 knots
Sci-fi/fantasy Reader? Gamer?	Read at 7 knots

TABLE OF CONTENTS

PRIOR TO PRE

1. from y to u

at approx. 210 knots

*I*n the beginning, there wasn't.

That's the thing. Well, ok: it's not necessarily *the* thing and it's almost necessarily not really a '*thing*' at all – if by '*thing*' you insist on a certain kind of definition: you know the kind. And you *know* you know, you know. You just don't *think* you know the kind because you don't know any other kind, so you think you don't know, when in fact you simply don't know you think.

Now you can look at me like I'm being unkind, like this is all my fault – on top of, beside and around being my problem. Do you really recall any moment of consciousness in which you settled comfortably into the auditions and decided just relax, accept and nauseatingly hug each next candidate for the meaning of thing. Yes, your preferred definitions tend to mind their own business and clean up after themselves. Yes, they tend to help most of our things stay the course as nice and concrete or nice and imaginable or, in any event, nice and seemingly straightforward kinds of objects (or aren't they more properly understood as subjects?). And oh yes indeed – oh I'm terribly sorry; did you think we were done? You most certainly do tend to forget or overlook or undersee the maddeningly elusive yet somehow simultaneously impenetrable word walls which trap, surround and *suffocate* just about every poor thing in the attempt.

I say – *we* say – that in the beginning there *wasn't* and I say – *we* say – that we're willing to compromise: Such observation or remark or conjecture or (darewesay) conclusion or (at the very least) viewpoint might, ok fair enough, not be *the* (one and only) thing, but it's as thingy as anything is – if ever a thinkworthy thing there was: Sure, it's a quiet little comment and lacks volume; it is nonetheless an incomparably enormous crescendo of a point. Right, of course, it comes without scriptural support and without mass; it nonetheless weighs (like noelse thing) so heavily on my mind and on my spirit – on *our* minds and spirits. Yes: It's of no matter; yet, I plead you consider, what off Earth could impossibly matter more?

In the beginning there wasn't and that recognition is a least *some*thing (can we compromise on that?) that, well, … let me just put it this way:

I cannot tell you how much more clarity in the world there would be if I – *we* – could get just a couple of people to go back to the "In the…" and begin to misunderstand that part a little more properly.

Eh? Surely I must mean 'start to *understand* that part…'? Well, no—

not quite… no. By which I intend to convey yes—why certainly, yes, by all means and without a doubt with all my heart but obviously, if you're asking which I'm answering, then no—not even remotely: I mean, I'd hardly snub the possibility of course – no more than I'd toss a winning lottery receipt into an evening ticker-tape parade, what am I now, some lunatic? A couple of people actually starting and properly no less *to understand?* Well, that would be blinding clarity assured, most assuredly, a wisdom feast, a comprehension banquet, a diploma day for all, now wouldn't it; indeed I'd be quite the fool not to dream of or at least allow for a chance at that pot of gold at the end of the iron-pyrite polychrome.

But that's not explicitly what I meant, no, dear me, I wouldn't dare: I mean, I am hardly in a position to presume that I properly *understand*, hardly in a position to suggest, in fact, that I've ever met anybody who does: maybe the effervescent **Ox** himself, but if so, he'd deny it. Maybe some of those of greater magnitude (those out in the appellate zones, for example), but how would I – how would *we* – presume to understand what they understand, without somehow hinting that there could be anything they did not understand and do you really take me to be as foolish as that would look?[2]

So… a couple more people actually understanding, sure. Sign me up.

---

[2] Come to think of it, as long as we're recklessly speculating, why don't I just go all-out and take it upon myself to muse upon the inner workings and weaknesses of the two just and merciless branch brigades of the **aaaPrioriii Special Ops**? How well done that would have been and now, blast it, how well done in I am. If not now careful: Having made the casual reference, obvious 'as if' though it may have been, I have no choice but to spell out and take back, to wit, as per, no less (et al.) the following: Any accidental suggestion or implication by omission of even the slightest deviation from perceptive perfection among the imperial asymptotic ranks of, you know, the **August Sisters of the Modus Ponen** or from, yes it should have gone without saying, the **Noble Brothers of the Domus Nopen**, is hereby regretted, retracted, repudiated and regarded repulsively. Really.

I dare not even imagine the joyous translucency I -- *we* -- would all experience. Never mind the thrill were I to be counted among they – *we* -- who understand.

But surely we should – *would* – settle for misunderstanding. Settle, my eye! – settle, *our we!* – it's the one and only reasonable objective to pursue! Misunderstanding, at least for the short-term, is, in fact, the goal. In the immediate, it's the purpose. With respect to the *now* – with all due respect to the *here-and* – it's the aim. All of which is to say: It's the thing.

Oh, that thing thing *again*? Don't be so smug. So what I'm a polarity packrat (*aficionado* of axes, thank you) with a hyper-shed full of obsolete and dilapidated dimensions, directions even, that doesn't mean I'm a whit less invested in moving *forward* and getting on with it already than are you. I'm also older, don't forget, so you might show a modicum of respect. Naturally, I don't necessarily mean older in *that* way but rather in the way we're trying – *I'm* trying – to, shall we say, expound, though indeed at this point I would delightedly settle for confound. Is it really that alienating when I call it *the thing*? Did I really forget to forewarn you or was it that, and I'm pretty sure it was, you forgot to forgive the phrase of turn?

OK, fine, I'll grant – *you* grant – it's something. And what it is is a single swarm of implications set in flight by the that which wasn't: the one which is all too frequently and so three strikingly and quite un-fortunately thought to have was'd '*in the beginning*' when it so couldn't have possibly was'd that we'd start lessening the madness right from the will-have-started if we'd realize what's not what and refer to it (to the *something* at hand) with a shred of accuracy and call it the that-whichn't or the thantn't. But you don't even care for the term *the thing*, though for different reasons, to be sure.

Let's call the ontological stinger at the center of this swarm, then, the Queen (not to) Be—just provisionally, if you'll indulge: just so that we're both clear on what we're talking about as the talking about grows increasingly unclear. Right now I'm just saying, as I was saying, about how I cannot tell you how much more clarity in the world there would be if I – *we* – could get just a couple of people to go back to the "In the…" and begin to misunderstand that part a little more properly.

The nature of the beast that is the Queen (not to) is simply (and hardly uniquely) this: It's far better misunderstood or even un-understood upon active considering than unconsidered upon passive overstanding.

Come now: This is nothing terribly new nor newly terrible. Look: It's a tricky set of ideas and, like all tricky sets worth having to the party in your mind, the most obvious way to mistreat them is to deny an invitation. And that's the obvious mistreatment but it's also the obvious course of action. Followed by most. Most won't even acknowledge, won't even shoot a glance in the direction, won't insult nor indulge (won't even ignore because that takes some kind of will or willfulness or at least willingness), won't even await awareness of – you know, any other way of starting the will-have-begun. The oblivion to the something, or really the violent push against the nothing, to the whole wasn't that was before the befores were already too late, is uberwhelming.

If even a couple people could start even to think about it, take it seriously enough to ponder, even invite the general topic into their consideration for long and deep enough to tolerate the inevitably exhilarating and enlightening and provocative confusions and, right, now you see, misunderstandings that inevitably must and do follow like leaders, well -- you see don't you? -- We could hardly pursue a loftier goal.

DOCKET 101

1. from Ox:

to enter & incorporate

at approx. 3 knots

 roceedings of the Infinity Court

For the 3rd Loop, Axis 18

Session Beginning February 2017

The Hon. Ox the Effervescent, Presiding

Docket 101, S17

1. Now before this court,

to enter and incorporate into the record for Docket 101.S17, being
the session beginning February 2017 and ending May 2017, and having
assigned without exception all available session hours to the hearing and
settling of the matter named below, a single action of no small weight nor
passing concern to this court, let this here now be notice from certified
diary that distributed at regular intervals throughout the above described
session to come,

There come Ten Motions.

The court will hear separately these ten motions and so render
separately its opinions. It prepares, as in the normal course, to call on
representation for the petitioners and on the characteristically wide array of
witnesses, lay and expert, to which this court humbly declares debt for its
great and unmatched repute. This court also prepares to invite, in
deliberate and emphasized exercise of its faculty to do so, briefs from any
and all 'friends' of the court (amicus), owing to the highly particular and
grave nature, admitted above, of a sole matter which finally joins into a
single trajectory then ten otherwise distinct motions to come before us.

2. Ever the way of this Court: As long as a motion be one of
which the court finds favor, then any relation or declaration found therein
shall be by writ adopted and absorbed into executive annals; all terms of the
motion to avail henceforth as reference, guidance and/or compulsion in the
settling of future questions involving matters of similar or related concern.
A motion here so granted thus becomes, unless and until it be reversed by

18

equivalent proceedings, a wholly assimilated element of the body and history of this court's rulings – bearing no less weight and no more scrutiny than any other like element. All such elements together comprise the sole source of precedent and common law appertaining to the settling of future matters within the jurisdiction and endowed with the full authority of any such element, once having been so integrated for any duration whatever.

What we find for (e.g.:) Motion #3 is therefore expressly subject to consultation and application in any question regarding (e.g.:) Motion #4; in no manner whatsoever, however, may we refer to Motion #4 when engaged in consideration of Motion #3.

3. *All Ten Motions are brought before this Court,*

in the order brought, so as to perform associated and cumulative functions – the full collection of which together constitute, this court is given by counsel to understand, one large and intricate argument being advanced by the defendant – in the one large and intricate matter now, and for all the remaining session, before this court.

The encompassing matter to which Docket 101 of the *Infinity Court* for the 3rd Loop now and for the remaining session dedicates its full attention is the swift and equitable settling of the question raised by counsel for the plaintiffs in:

"*People vs. Earth*",   in which

a double-wide celestial sphere had long been under stellar surveillance – due largely to its association with elements (e.g.: oxygen, silicon and iron) that are widely believed to forge bonds and show traces to the powerful *crystollegen* and *chalcogen* families or 'groups'. Recently, the suspect was flagged down by Officer Sidereus Simplicio of the 18th Axis. The suspect, described itself as a 'mobile home' and insisted that it was 'as innocent as the day is long'. Documentation legally identified the suspect as *Terra "Earth" Firma*. Officer Simplicio alleges that *Earth* was in clear excess of the speed limit posted in the zone for spheres of its type.

According to the report he filed, Officer Simplicio followed standard procedure and visibly presented a badge, a cotton weave bandage as well as his personal (prized) pair of lucky fuzzy quantum dice. Reportedly, therefore, the officer's subsequent search of the sphere was prompted by demonstration of probable gauze; the search uncovered revealed that '*Earth*' to be carrying suspiciously high volumes of water, many of which were not stowed properly. To the possession charge Earth has pleaded no contest, but the alleged moving violation which prompted the search is the matter now before the court.

Officer Simplicio has issued a summons to *Earth*
for excessive and reckless violation
of a velocity that was
(1) plainly publicized as a legal limit
        and
(2) historically verified as a safety requirement.

Attend we now; presently, we shall ask:
T. "Earth" Firma, you have been charged with:

One count: Tending toward revolution   &
One count: Exceeding the clear and cosmic speed limit of
      Zero.

How do you plead?

In light of the matter's gravity,

This court feels duty-bound to remind all who observe:
This court has been, as was averred above,

broadly recognized for its
singularly thorough,
scientifically objective and ethically enlightened
administrating of justice.

By such acknowledgment, this court is only further humbled
And prepared to undertake its present duties,
In service of its role

As 3rd –to-highest in the chain of appeals
For the jurisprudential structure serving loop 3, Axis 18

of all
United F.R. Traffic Courts.

Electron bless the United F of R
Submitted this day,
The Hon: Ox the Effervescent,
Loop 3, Axis 18.

2. witness: in re Earth

One who speaks, hears, understands
and knows,
One who speaks, hears and
understands,
One who hears and understands;
i.e.: a three who look and see.

1ST. SUN

J esse, Missy Jean and Professor Piyopiyo lived on a land

called "Earth." Earth was a big land, divided into many smaller places. Their place was called "40 degrees North of the Equator; 74 degrees West of the Prime Meridian." Their time was called "The first day of Autumn."

Once again, it was late at night. Thrillingly late. So late somehow that a little later and soon it would be early in the morning, way before the afternoon. It was never fully clear how that part ever fully worked. Once again, Jesse, Missy Jean and Prof. Piyopiyo were in the laboratory on 4, near the corner of 10 and 59, in the building named T of John J. Once again, Missy Jean was at the counter working on a secret potion. This time, thus far, the potion involved sodium bicarbonate, yoghurt, ice chips and a few iron filings. The potion did not yet do what it was supposed to do. It was, however, unusually magnetic for something so tasty.

Jesse was on the floor studying how rattles and small stuffed animals behaved when he did not put them in his mouth. Jesse had very recently started to make observations under this challenging condition. His observations were still limited. He was fairly convinced that stuffed animals, when kept away from his mouth, were neither tasty nor magnetic.

Prof. Piyopiyo was at his desk. Without looking, Missy Jean just knew it. And she knew what he was doing: scribbling symbol after symbol—all somehow neat and yet unreadable at the same time—in that thick brown journal of unlined paper. He called the symbols "math," but Missy Jean knew better.

Missy Jean had learned "math" last year in her school. Her school was called 92-Street-Y. Her class had finished all of math in time for summer and she even got her big-sticker sheets right. So Missy Jean knew what math was all about: numbers. Whatever symbols covered Prof. Piyopiyo's unlined sheets, they certainly were not numbers.

Prof. Piyopiyo looked at his watch. He looked at Jesse and he looked at Missy Jean. He said, "Let's go outside and see something beautiful." Nobody wished to argue this plan. Missy Jean put on her shoes. Prof. Piyopiyo scooped Jesse off the floor. They went outside, hailed a cab and stood on the edge of the Drive called F-D-R.

The three looked off to what Prof. Piyopiyo called the "East." A sphere of blazing crimson was rising magnificently behind three buildings near two bridges that came from one short place. The place melted off into a mysterious island that Prof. Piyopiyo called "Long". Right now, it was too long to see and too wide to cross, but it all grew out and left, if Jesse heard Prof. Piyopiyo right, from a blue part called the "Sound". Jesse was a little confused by this name; all the ups and overs and outs and colors seemed so nice—so slow and silent. Cool and quiet, not like a sound, but also not like a picture. Not at all like one of those pictures you could hold in your hand on a buzzing phone. No, watching the sunrise was more like sitting on the couch with Missy Jean and a peaceful movie—but lost in cushions made of clouds and no reasons to rewind. Things were calm and clear with Missy Jean. She even knew how to spell movie: "D-V-D". He was proud.

2ND. MOON

*B*efore pajama time, Jesse was aware of the dusty,

dusky traces of sunlight. Were they coming or going? At the lab, Jesse
found Missy Jean. She too was looking forward to another sunrise. Finally,
Prof. Piyopiyo said, "Let's bring our suppers outside and see if the sun rises
again."

And so they did, but so it didn't.

Instead, they saw the moon—far higher than the place in which they had recently found the sun. The moon was bright and beautiful, but looked like someone had bitten it. Half of it was missing.

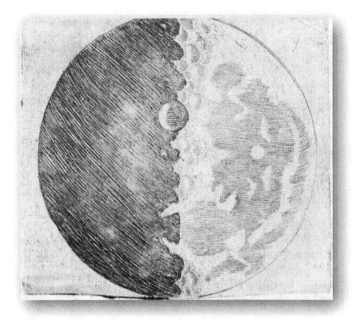

The Moon (Galileo, 1610; public domain)

The three remained quiet for a long time after the stars faded from view and the sun dominated the low sky. The whole thing was indeed a movie. Both the fading stars and the rising sun trekked from one sky edge to on their way to the other. It appeared as though Missy Jean, Prof. Piyopiyo and Jesse were under a big round tent. Somebody invisible was pulling the tent top from left to right. At last, it dawned on Missy Jean: "It might be nice to see that again some time."

"Why?" thought Jesse. He remembered one night when the moon looked like a perfect circle. He remembered it well because the moon kept following him around that night—even when he was in his car-seat zooming up that same FDR Drive. What kind of creature would eat his moon?

Jesse thought and Missy Jean asked. Prof. Piyopiyo assured them:

"Don't you worry. The moon's still there. Part of it is just hidden in shadow. The moon cannot make its own light the way the sun can.

Sunlight bounces off the moon and heads toward our eyes. Sometimes more gets bounced, sometimes less. Depends where the moon is."

Supper was long, leisurely and quiet. Missy Jean was deep in her mashed potatoes. Jesse was deep in thought: How do some things 'make their own light'? The sun did, but the moon didn't? Did he? Did Missy Jean? Prof. Piyopiyo probably did: He certainly made a lot of his own noise.

3RD. STARS

"W hat about the stars?"

asked Missy Jean. "Why can't we go say hello to them before we say good night to ourselves?"

"Why not indeed?" replied Prof. Piyopiyo. The three walked outside and Prof. Piyopiyo pointed up.

"See that sideways V that looks like a mouth? It's head of a bull named 'Taurus'. That bright red giant star, Aldeberan, is its eye."

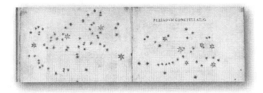

Stars (staying arranged in familiar shapes, such as Taurus the Bull)

Missy Jean and Jesse loved animals. They kept their eyes on the bull for a long, long time. Long enough, it turned out, to notice that it, like all the animals and fish and twins and hunters and everything else around it, it seemed, slid smoothly across the sky—from down and left to up and center to down and right, it seemed.

"Good job, world," said Missy Jean, "Just keep on turning around us like that."

"Yes. Good job, world," thought Jesse.

"Good night, you two," declared Prof. Piyopiyo
"The early bird catches the worm".

Missy Jean was not so interested in catching a worm, but Jesse had no strong feelings on the matter. His eyelids dropped fully by the word "bird". Somehow, he later found himself in bed.

4TH. VENUS

The next evening, the three rushed outside and

zoomed over to the Hudson River to see if they could catch the sun setting in what Prof. Piyopiyo called "the west". There was a big tugboat blocking their view. Sadly, it seemed that they had arrived too late.

Happily, however, they arrived just in time to see the biggest, brightest star they had ever noticed. It seemed be setting—just like they had been hoping for the sun. "Wow; dazzling," thought Jesse.

Venus (following the sun, wandering off the canopy of steady constellations)

"Is that super-duper star always to the right of Taurus?" asked Missy Jean.

"Actually, no," explained Prof. Piyopiyo "That thing wanders back and forth--but always stays near the sun. It wanders past the bull, the ram, the scorpion and the other nine animals who march together across the southern sky. Because it wanders, it's actually called a 'planet.'

"It's the planet Venus," finished Prof. Piyopiyo Jesse suddenly felt different from how he had a moment ago. He had been excited-happy and now he was calm-happy. It was funny how having a name for something memorable seemed to solve a mystery. It was also funny how a mystery's solution could create its own confusion: Which was more fun—searching or finding?

5TH. JUPITER

he next night involved more searching and more

finding. The three went out far later than they had on previous nights.

After this evening's dinner (juicy chicken to eat and chickeny juice to drink), they played and sang and danced and danced and sang and played for tons of time before heading out to the edge of the valley. The sun was long gone; Venus was long gone. Even Taurus was getting close to that mountain in the west.

But up in the sky, amongst the connect-the-dot crab that Prof. Piyopiyo called "Cancer", blazed another unusually bright star—almost as big and beautiful as Venus.

Neither Missy Jean nor Jesse failed to notice. How could they? Prof. Piyopiyo did not fail to answer their unasked question:

"You got it, guys: Another planet. That one is Jupiter. Planets aren't always that bright, but they do always move dance to their own tune. Some day, some year, you won't find Jupiter among the crab stars. You'll find it among the lines of the lion or the specks of the sea-goat."

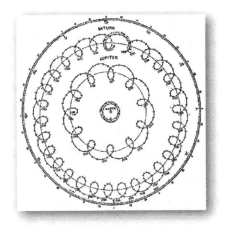

Jupiter (also wandering at its own speed; sometimes dramatically changing direction)

6TH. PHASES OF VENUS

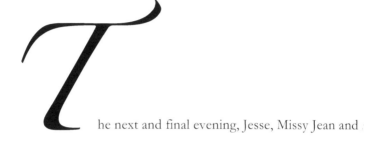

he next and final evening, Jesse, Missy Jean and

Prof. Piyopiyo rushed out early in order to try and catch the sun before it dropped behind the big mountain. Again, they missed it. It was too bad, but not too too bad. Neither Jesse nor Missy Jean truly wanted to win in a competition against Mother Nature or Father Time.

Any disappointment they might have felt disappeared the moment Prof. Piyopiyo pulled two small but clunky black objects from his bag. Each object was a pair of binoculars. Jesse and Missy Jean each gazed toward the mountain through the long, thick glasses. Suddenly, it seemed as though they had stepped a dozen times closer to outer space.

Without the binoculars, they spotted and recognized Venus. With the binoculars, a bit of confusion set in.

Missy Jean spoke: "Now Venus looks like the moon!"

Jesse knew what she meant. Now that he was closer to Venus, it no longer looked like a wandering star. Like the moon, this circle was missing a chunk.

Venus through a Telescope (presenting different shapes, or 'phases', in the manner of our moon)

So some sky-wanderers did not make their own light?

Prof. Piyopiyo nodded as though he had heard Jesse's thought.

38

Instead of answering, he asked a different question:

"Missy Jean, do you think the firm ground below you makes its own light?"

Missy Jean replied with confidence, "No silly; dirt isn't fire!"

"Makes sense to me," stated Prof. Piyopiyo. Made sense to Jesse, also.

7TH. MOONS OF JUPITER

*I*ndeed, at some times, some space things were starting to

seem clearer to Jesse. Yet he was surprised to find—at some other times—that the more he looked at some other other things, the less clear the other other other things seemed to seem. If some sky-wanderers did not make their own light, and if Earth did not make its own light, did that mean Earth was like a sky-wanderer? It certainly did not feel that way.

If circles were shapes, for example, did that mean that shapes were circles? It certainly did not seem that way.

Yet something about those wanderers made Jesse feel a bit dizzier in his mind and even dizzier on his feet.

To make matters more surprising, Prof. Piyopiyo then pulled four objects out of his pack: three large and one small, but all squishy. Jesse loved that pack. He loved how it was bigger on the inside than it was on the outside.

Prof. Piyopiyo unrolled the three large objects. They were sleeping bags.

But neither Missy Jean nor Jesse noticed until later. They noticed the small squishy bag. It had marshmallows.

Prof. Piyopiyo explained: "Let's make a fire, roast marshmallows and sleep under the stars. I'll wake you when Jupiter comes out."

They did and he did.

Jesse and Missy Jean found Jupiter. Jupiter wasn't quite as sharp as Venus, but Jupiter was bold. Jupiter wore an orange robe. Jupiter was king. It sat solemnly on a floating throne.

Prof. Piyopiyo offered last night's "binoculars": those long black eyes that had shown them Venus's missing piece. Jesse twitched. Sure, he liked finding new things that were there—especially when they were hard to see. But last night's hollow bite from Venus was still eating at him. How had Prof. Piyopiyo pointed out something that *wasn't* there—something that before had seemed so easy to see?

They clutched on and took giant steps toward Jupiter—through their new and superpower eyes. When they stared at Jupiter, it was more and so seemed closer. But when they stared at its black surrounding realm, that too was more and yet seemed farther. Their balance grew weaker; their vision grew stronger.

Soon, in a line surrounding Jupiter, four brand new stars fuzzed into view.

"Wow," exclaimed Missy Jean, delighting in her discovery, "Space is even bigger on the inner of its outer than I think I might have thought."

Jupiter through a telescope (evidently trailing four of its own wanderers, each looping tightly around it in the manner of our moon)

"Oy," thought Jesse.

"Are those regular stars or sky-wanderers?" asked Missy Jean, sorting out her discovery.

Prof. Piyopiyo replied: "Oh, those four wander all right. But they don't just wander around. They wander around Jupiter. Those are four of Jupiter's moons."

A world of worlds going around a world—inside the biggest world of all?

Jesse's thoughts swirled. They whirled.

Jesse thought he had a funny feeling, but he did not feel he had a funny thought.

"So, a thing in the sky can go around a thing in the sky that goes around a . . . ?" cried Missy Jean. She slapped a hand on her own mouth— to keep at least her sentence from running away toward forever. So much was slipping. Super-slick yet somehow steadily.

"And so, a heavy rock can fly like light—and wander through the dark of space?" wondered Jesse.

"The Earth feels so still, and . . . ," started Missy Jean.

"… and still it moves," saw Jesse.

* * *

And as Jesse thought this thought, he too moved:

this time through time. . . toward the future.

He grew older.

Perhaps, you might say, but only by a minute or two and only at the speed of life.

Yes, but this time, he felt it.

3. game play

at approx. 7 knots

USER's GUIDE

to

Infinity Court

Now... in BOARD GAME format...

'SMALL CLAIMS' v2.0!

For all our precious Travelin' Tots & Prime Movers!

Moms & Dads, premember!
Our precious little particles are radiating –
whether we're ready or not!
We can't be around to co-occupy every eigenstate they manifest.

You did your first job and kept them safe from the world:
now do your second job and teach them how to navigate its dangers & shadier zones –
but gently, at home, while having fun!

Premember! The earlier we can get our precious quarks and muons to take controlled risks
and build their infinity-immunities to reality's rougher regions
then it's just a lighter load for all!
Have courage! Show your the young 'uns what can happen between 'space' and 'time'
before they hear about it on the street!

Pick up and play:

'SMALL CLAIMS' (v2.0) (before the) *Infinity Court*

Available in Compact & EZ-Play
Version 2.0: Total game-play guaranteed for as few as 1.81 dimensions!

And now... game on!
Quickstart Guide on Next Page!

QUICKSTART

1. The hypothesis:

You are **HERE*** :

*stuck on the corner in a shady part of town:
stuck and lost in a rough neighborhood which swirls around
the intersection of 'space' and 'time'.

All the locals You are at a point known by the natives as

2. The Challenge:

Get **THERE*** :

*to a point of infinite reward known by the natives as

47

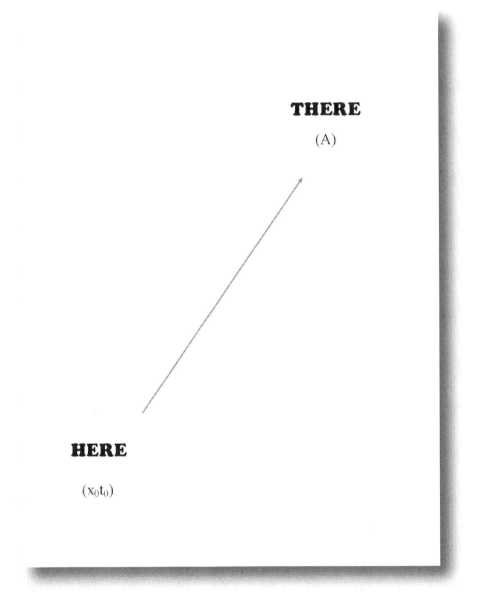

THERE

(A)

HERE

$(x_0 t_0)$

For tips on expert game play or help with the higher dimensions, please see the complete and comprehensive manual, aka 'the book':

Pre-Trial Motions Before the Infinity Court.

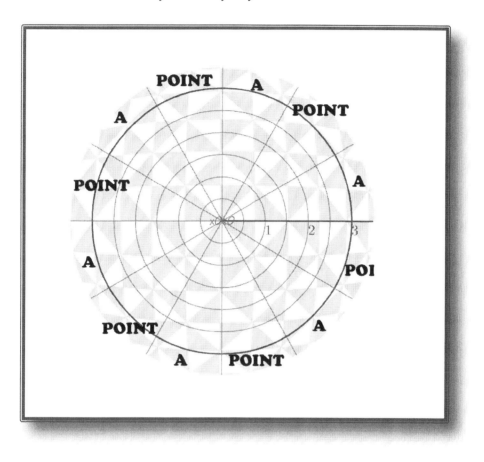

For a tip on how to endure or follow 'the book' (*Pre-Trial Motions...),*

Remember:

Students:	**Read at 32 knots**
Lawyers:	**Read at 40 knots**
Graduate faculty:	**Read at 92 knots**

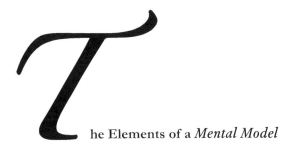

4. *of models to muse*

at approx. **5** knots

*T*he Elements of a *Mental Model*

Particularly since findings driven by the *Force Concept Inventory* (Halloun

& Hestenes, 1985; Hestenes & Swackhammer, 1992), techniques regarding the construction and communication of mental models have been moving toward the center of progressive physics pedagogy (Jackson, Dukerich & Hestenes, 2008, p. 111).

In the development and practice of science, the elements of a theory often function as predictive representations, rather than as creeds or ontological claims. Descartes, for example, invited readers to accept his fresh scientific descriptions not as "postulates representing his own beliefs but as useful models from which one could deduce consequences in agreement with observations" (Etkina, Warren & Gentile, 2006, p. 34). In the contemporary context of physics instruction, Hestenes has defined a scientific model as a "surrogate object—a conceptual representation of the real thing" (Hestenes, 1987, p. 441). This root definition has been deployed and developed through physics curricula at varying levels of formality.

Currently, a typical physics model is generally characterized by the following three elements (adapted from Etkina, Matilsky & Lawrence, 2003):

1. *A physics model* is a rich analogy to a physical phenomenon or principle.

2. The analogy deliberately trades certain aspects of descriptive completeness for certain gains in descriptive simplicity.

3. The ultimate purpose of the analogy is predictive power.

Mental Models and Physics Cognition

The processes by which people learn physics are necessarily related to the processes by which people think about physics. The general character of a mental model has origins in cognitive literature. Two of these cognitive s inform the particular role played by models in the study suggested

ɔaper.

Models of motion. Literature concerning *mental animation* (Hegarty, 1992) and *analog imagery* (Schwartz and Black, 1996) demonstrates that predictively strong comprehension of mechanical sequences often involves a thread of smoothly connected mental pictures. In analyzing a system of pulleys or gears, for example, people appear to internalize some sort of primitive movie for which the frames are linked to one another by causality. If the mental movie is conceived properly, it will continue running even after the observed data have run their course: the movie's finale serves as a prediction for the empirical world. These dynamic mental models have been found to flow from a definite point of view or perspective. In a text-oriented study performed by Black, Turner and Bower (1976), reading times were longer for sentences of the form "Terry finished working in the yard and he came into the house" than they were for "Terry finished working in the yard and he went into the house". The thought-train derailment and resulting delay were attributed to a kind of mental picture- story that went awry at the moment of a seeming inconsistency in perspective:

In our camera metaphor, the switched sentence requires that the camera set be struck, moved inside, and set up again to film the action. This takes time and effort, and interrupts the smooth flow of comprehension. If the interruption is too costly, the critical sentence may be "rewritten" in the memory representation, transforming it to be consistent with the on-going point of view (Black, Turner & Bower, 1976, p. 189).

The point for this context is that a mental model involves more than a set of propositions: The two above sentences contain identical information, yet produce distinct cognitive reactions. A mental model, particularly one for a kinematic phenomenon, must contain some kind of visualization. This visualization, in turn, relies on a choice of vantage point or perspective.

Models of deduction. Mental models were introduced by Johnson-Laird (1983) as schemes by which people assimilated and tested the potential validity of syllogisms. Under this view, people who are faced with a set of propositions construct a mental list of all circumstances—or *possible worlds*—that are conceivable according to the propositions. In order to verify or derive a conclusion, they check to see if their imagined universe includes or produces the conclusion. According to Johnson-Laird, "a mental model represents a true possibility, and it represents a clause in the premises only when the clause is true in the possibility" (Holyoak & Morrison, 2005, p. 190). Here, the prediction facilitated by a mental model is not of a sense-accessible event, but of a logical conclusion. Like the Hegarty animation, the Johnson-Laird possible world involves a kind of narrative composed of something more or other than words. The causal links of a mental animation forces a conclusion while the modus ponens links of a possible world permit a conclusion.

Whether inductive or deductive in target, however, a mental model is a dynamic extended metaphor the end of which is prediction.

By applying its roots in cognition literature to the contemporary physics pedagogy context, our understanding of a model's essential elements (Etkina, Matilsky & Lawrence, 2003) can be refined. The analogy described above will not qualify as "rich" if it consists solely of words— particularly not if the analogy is intended to capture something from the observable world of space and time.

The kind of extended metaphor or representation described above, moreover, functions quite nicely, no doubt, in the case of an established, practiced and comfortable understanding. We can turn to mental models for assistance with new applications of familiar phenomena, such as: How high in the sky should I expect to find the sun at noon from this new latitude at which I just arrived? If, however, we are interested in the mental models held by people who are in the process of working out a new understanding, we need, perhaps, the addition of a distinguishing feature – one put in place to aid in the model's development rather than simply its use. In this curriculum and in this research, that extra element could be termed '*personal specificity*'. For a model to aid an individual student in the process of internalizing a new set of definitions, laws and techniques, it must contribute some level of translation or identification: A job of the model is to assist the smooth passage of some way of thinking from outside to inside a mental space; we might be asking such mental space to shift and change a bit so as to accommodate the new thoughts, but we should nonetheless expect to find the space characterized by some kind of shape. It seems reasonable and realistic to expect a limit past which such shape will not bend to accommodate a rigid model. To increase probability of cognitive impact, the model ought, it seems here, bear some of the flexibility burden; it ought to allow some tailoring to the mentality in which it is meant to dwell. For the context of physics and physics education research, the following operational definition for mental model is thus offered:

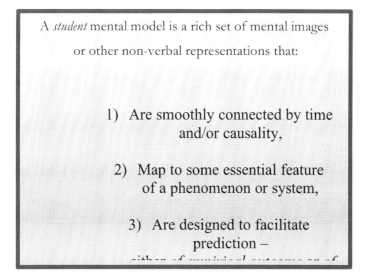

A *student* mental model is a rich set of mental images

or other non-verbal representations that:

1) Are smoothly connected by time
   and/or causality,

2) Map to some essential feature
   of a phenomenon or system,

3) Are designed to facilitate
   prediction –

Conceptual Change

The seminal work regarding the teaching of relativity was done by

Hewson (1982). Much of the contemporary research on classroom

treatment of reference frames and transformations refers to the notions of

conceptual change that were demonstrated in Hewson's 1982 paper (Hewson,

1992; Scherr, Shaffer, & Vokos, 2001; Villani, 1998). Such notions

undergird the theoretical framework for the study proposed by this paper.

The challenges entailed both by learning and by teaching relativity invite education models for conceptual change and a wealth of literature on the broader theory is available (Hewson & Hewson, 1984; Linn, 2006; Pintrich, Marx, & Boyle, 1993). Specific focus on relativity, however, does not saturate the field. Placement of relativity in the landscape of physics pedagogy tends to rely first on findings from Hewson that we discuss immediately below. In subsequent decades, relativity and related conceptual change research tended to emerge from either McDermott's Physics Education Research Group at the University of Washington (see, for example, O'Brien Pride, 1997) or Hestenes's Modeling Instruction Program at Arizona State University (see, for example, Hestenes, Wells & Swackhammer, 1992). A precedent for conceptual-change analysis of relativity pedagogy has been set, but, again, narrowly.

Metaphysical Commitments & Spontaneous Ways of Reasoning

Hewson performed a qualitative case study. He interviewed a graduate tutor for college freshman physics on three occasions separated in time. The object of interview investigation was the tutor's "metaphysical commitments" (Hewson, 1982, p. 61). He was asked about the sort of ontologies and claims that sat underneath his direct contemplation of physics problems—first in the abstract, second—in order to probe their durability—after four months had passed, and third, ten days later, after a discussion concerning Einstein's special theory of relativity had been woven through the second interview.

Known as *SL*, the tutor interviewed by Hewson had been selected for a particular reason: He had participated in a study of conceptual change and relativity that had been conducted earlier in the year by Hewson and colleagues: Posner, et al. (1982). There, Posner established the significance of *"metaphysical beliefs about science"* and *"metaphysical concepts of science"* (Posner, 1982, p. 215). In order to define the latter in the context of science education, the study notes that "concepts often have a metaphysical quality in that they are beliefs about the ultimate nature of the universe and are immune from direct empirical refutation. A belief in absolute space or time is an example" (p. 215). This definition, along with one for metaphysical beliefs in science, was applied in a qualitative investigation. In it, undergraduate students and professors were asked to solve two problems in special relativity and to provide 'think-aloud' responses to vocal questions while they proceeded through their solutions.

Both the forerunning Posner and the flagship Hewson study found that a mental background of non-verifiable postulates left a discernible impact on the way young physicists approach questions from modern topics. The studies found, moreover, that communication guided toward this metaphysical background helped improve analysis in the foreground.

Essential both to Hewson's study and to many conceptual change approaches is this premise: Authentic learning involves the transformation or replacement of misguided mental schema, rather than a simple insertion of fresh ones. That is, "prior knowledge" (p. 61) matters; effective pedagogy consciously accounts for the cognitive lens through which a student views the world before pedagogy is introduced.

A specific shape taken in physics by prior knowledge had been uncovered and named the *spontaneous* (or natural) *way of reasoning (SWR)* by Saltiel and Malgrange (p. 74, 1980). Their study posed two-dimensional problems involving motion viewed from two distinct perspectives (*reference frames*). The quantitative problems were presented both to 700 freshmen and seniors in university and to 80 eleven-year-old children. Between the two groups, the distribution of right and wrong solutions was found to be statistically significantly similar. Motion tends to seem like some kind of absolute property to people. Whether the people in question have yet to contemplate motion in a rigorous fashion, have formally considered the nuances of motion, or have been repeatedly trained in its non-absolute character, conclusions seem remarkably uniform. Recognition of the Aristotlean preconceptions with which pupils enter—and, all too often, leave—a physics class became a fundamental focus of the ASU Modeling Instruction Program (Halloun & Hestenes, 1985).

Prior to Einstein

Of particular consequence in this paper is the apparent resistance of SWR to relativistic scrutiny even before Einstein's special relativity is introduced: SWR seem to impede cognition regarding the principle of relativity in its foundational form. Next to the twentieth century context of time dilation, mass-energy equivalence, etc., Galilean relativity can appear deceptively straightforward. The examples provided by Kumar (1998), "… show that in physics teaching, it is wrong to dismiss Newtonian relativity as obvious. The naïve intuitive notions of the beginners need to be carefully changed to the correct repertoire of prescriptive notions of Newtonian relativity. All we can say is that this transition is not as difficult as that required by Einstein's relativity." The non-obvious implication of the first repertoire, to be discussed more thoroughly below, is at the core of the study here proposed.

In more recent studies, direct confrontation of prior knowledge remains a fundamental part of the conceptual change agenda—specifically as it plays out in the realm of science education. From McCloskey (1983) to

Nersessian (1992) to Thornton (1997), the evolution of tacit beliefs concerning mechanics have been traced and treated. A countable few studies, however, have been particularly geared toward Galilean inertial reference frames (or coordinate systems) and their equivalence.

With the Group at Washington, Scherr, Shaffer and Vokos (2001) conducted a vast investigation spanning five years and 800 undergraduate students. Students at varying levels of exposure solved problems in special relativity and participated in hour-long interviews. The topic of simultaneity underlay the problems. As with the studies mentioned above, findings emphasized powerful currents of thinking which permeate problem-solving independent of, prior to and, in some cases, even after instruction. Scherr, et al. concluded:

Special relativity offers instructors an opportunity to channel student interest in modern physics into a challenging intellectual experience. For most people, the implications of special relativity are in strong conflict with their intuition. For students to recognize the conflict and appreciate its resolution, they need to have a functional understanding of some very basic concepts. . . This investigation documents prevalent modes of reasoning with these fundamental concepts as a first step toward making special relativity meaningful to students (Scherr, Shaffer & Vokos, 2001, p. S34).

In the context of this study, "basic concepts" referred to tenets such as the local nature of measurement. This understanding achieves profound vitality under Einstein's *general* theory of relativity, but did not have agency in the Galilean scheme. The concepts probed by Scherr, et al. were at the base of an edifice built, perhaps, a steppe or two above sea level.

The application of conceptual change techniques to relativity appears to have slowed in the early nineties. Examination of prior knowledge continues, nonetheless, to play a critical role in science education research. Among the more contemporary and influential papers on conceptual change was completed by Linn (2006). It underscored the revelatory potential of pre-instruction thought processes. According to Linn, a number of varied "research programs suggest that students develop a repertoire that includes ideas that are sound, contradictory, confused, idiosyncratic, arbitrary, and based on flimsy evidence. The way students justify and organize their ideas reveals their epistemology of science, beliefs about learning, and views of scientists" (p. 247).

A teacher whose strategies are guided by a conceptual change model will endeavor not simply to teach the new, but, rather, to un-teach the old. The topic of relativity pertains to objects and agents with which people at all developmental stages have familiarity: Horses, boats, volleyballs and planets enter the discussion far earlier than do sub-atomic particles or electromagnetic waves. It is the conclusion, not the focus, of relativity that runs counter to common intuitions regarding how things move. The presence of an intuition threatened by the prospect of dissonance is precisely what summons a theoretical framework of conceptual change. A worthy teaching of relativity, that is, demands a robust recognition of anisotropy (or whatever interpretation stands in relativity's way).

Mental Models and Relativity

As was explained earlier in this paper, models are used and studied with vivid results in modern physics classrooms. As was explained prior to that, comprehension of the *principle of relativity* is crucial for success in modern physics curricula. The core problem is that these two basic findings are rarely brought together in physics pedagogy. The study described by this paper seeks to expand the comparatively small literary

60

body of modeling approaches for relativity instruction.

In the study here described, student mental models regarding inertial reference frames and velocity were collected over a series of stages through an undergraduate course in calculus- based classical mechanics. These mental models were analyzed in the context of a course that covers the traditional topics, yet has been deliberately reconfigured so as to place explicit and repeated emphasis on Galileo's *principle of relativity* as the theoretical and thematic framework. Analysis is both quantitative and qualitative.

DOCKET
102

5. from Ox:

to enter & incorporate

at approx. 3 knots

roceedings of the Infinity Court

For the 3ʳᵈ Loop, Axis 18
Session Beginning February 2017
The Hon. Ox the Effervescent, Presiding
Docket 102, S17

1.   Now before this court,

to enter and incorporate into the record for Docket 102.S17, being
the session beginning February 2017 and ending May 2017, and having
assigned without exception all available session hours to the hearing and
settling of the matter named below, a single action of no small weight nor
passing concern to this court, let this here now be notice from certified
diary that distributed at regular intervals throughout the above described
session to come,

There come *Ten Motions.*

The court will hear separately these ten motions and so render
separately its opinions. It prepares, as in the normal course, to call on
representation for the petitioners and on the characteristically wide array of
witnesses, lay and expert, to which this court humbly declares debt for its
great and unmatched repute. This court also prepares to invite, in
deliberate and emphasized exercise of its faculty to do so, briefs from any
and all 'friends' of the court (amicus), owing to the highly particular and
grave nature, admitted above, of a sole matter which finally joins into a
single trajectory then ten otherwise distinct motions to come before us.

2.   Ever the way of this Court: As long as a motion be one of
which the court finds favor, then any relation or declaration found therein
shall be by writ adopted and absorbed into executive annals; all terms of the
motion to avail henceforth as reference, guidance and/or compulsion in the
settling of future questions involving matters of similar or related concern.

A motion here so granted thus becomes, unless and until it be reversed by equivalent proceedings, a wholly assimilated element of the body and history of this court's rulings – bearing no less weight and no more scrutiny than any other like element. All such elements together comprise the sole source of precedent and common law appertaining to the settling of future matters within the jurisdiction and endowed with the full authority of any such element, once having been so integrated for any duration whatever.

What we find for (e.g.:) Motion #3 is therefore expressly

subject to consultation and application

in any question regarding (e.g.:) Motion #4;

in no manner whatsoever, however,

may we refer to Motion #4

when engaged in consideration of Motion #3.

3.   *All Ten Motions are brought before this Court,*

in the order brought, so as to perform associated and cumulative functions – the full collection of which together constitute, this court is given by counsel to understand, one large and intricate argument being advanced by the defendant – in the one large and intricate matter now, and for all the remaining session, before this court.

The encompassing matter to which Docket 102 of the *Infinity Court* for the 3rd Loop now and for the remaining session dedicates its full attention is the swift and equitable settling of the question raised by counsel for the plaintiffs in:

"*Region IV vs. Boundary III*",

aka

in which

the edge of the known universe

was flagged down by Officer i.j. Manifold of the 13th geodesic.
Officer Manifold identified himself but received no cooperation.
He ultimately issued a summons to the edge

for spreading in the wrong direction down a one-way vector
and speeding up upon being advised to pull over.

The *Edgeofthe Universe* was subsequently arraigned;
It has been read its tensor transformations
and comes here before us.
Attend we now; Presently, we shall ask:

T.E. Universe, you have been charged with:
One count of EXPANDING &
one count of ACCELERATING
while expanding.

How do you plead?

In light of the matter's gravity,

This court feels duty-bound to remind all who observe:
This court has been, as was averred above,

broadly recognized for its

singularly thorough,

scientifically objective and ethically enlightened

administrating of justice.

By such acknowledgment, this court is only further humbled

And prepared to undertake its present duties,

In service of its role

As 3rd —to-highest in the chain of appeals

For the jurisprudential structure serving loop 3, Axis 18

of all

United F.R. Traffic Courts.

Electron bless the United F of R

Submitted this day,

The Hon: Ox the Effervescent,

Loop 3, Axis 18

6. from Ox to Clocks

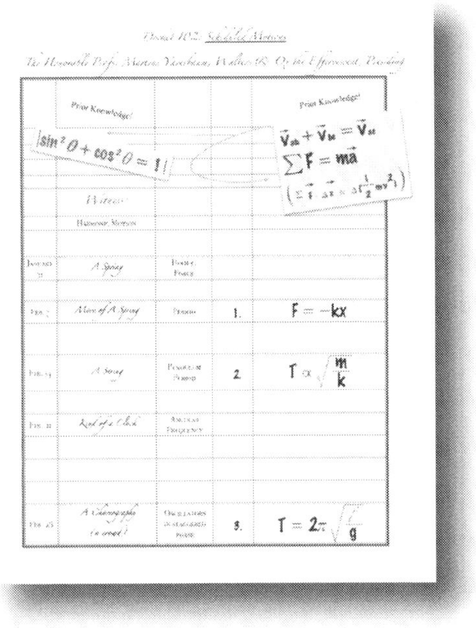

Module 7	THE Td.	Propagation along a 1-D medium	4.	$x - x_0\cos(\omega t) + \rho$
	Standing Wave Motion			
Module 14	A Pattern (of Patterns) PART	Standing Waves on a 2-D medium		
	Motion of Loaded			
Module 21	Two Reference Frames and a Medium: THE Effect. PART	Doppler Effect for Sound	5.	$\Delta L = \dfrac{n\lambda}{2}$
	Momentum & Distance			
Module 28	Seas ices and a compass needle: A perspective from Earth	Bar Magnets	6.	$v = \dfrac{\omega}{K}$

69

APRIL 4	Cut for end of glass rod. THE Field	ELECTROSTATIC FIELD & MAGNETIC FIELD		
		MOTION IN A CIRCUIT		
APRIL 25	Adopt	DRIFT VELOCITY IN A WIRE	7.	$E = \pm \dfrac{\overline{K}Q_1}{r^2}$
MAY 2	A Variation	LC CIRCUITS	8.	$\Delta V = IR$
		MOTION OF LIGHT		
MAY 9	Two Slits. THE Unification	YOUNG INTERFERENCE OF LIGHT		
MAY 16	A shift @ THE Question	HUBBLE'S LAW	9.	$\Delta L = \dfrac{n\lambda}{2}$
MAY 18	Exam Review		10.	$v = H_0 r$
MAY 25	Final (Hour) EXAM			8.30 pm - 9.30 pm

70

7. witness: in re a spring

(b) at approx. 40 knots

 (said he -- that is, Huque -- that is, the witness in re a

spring) cannot recall what business I had there or with whom, but I know it was mine and though I didn't mind it a bit, no sir, if there is one thing I do know it's that it was I 'twas minding it and only 'twas it I was to mind. The whole, nothing but the, all and only: I warn't doing nothing but minding my own business – sure I'm sure. Then I saw, not for looking you understand, but for lack of knack not to and plus my business demanded it – though precisely for what I seem now to forget. I saw it plain as day and that's the part I'll ever recollect, but only and very simply because you understand there was really nothing to recollect. Same as always: No difference to make a difference: From minding my very own business and with my very own busy eyes, I saw it:

A regular ordinary trusted and solid block of mass (m) was fixed to one end of a very, very well-behaved spring: All around a straightforward and steady pair.

Of course, we're not saying perfect, understand: These were real objects under dwelling under real rulers and clocks – bound for uncertainty like all the rest: some error too. But good and reliable things they were: By every account and at every data table, that spring was as faithful and law-abiding as they come. Now we're talking about what matters and what's matter which numbers really count and when we're talking about a spring, then it's **Hooke's Law** first and last:

Sure that spring would deviate a bit, get a little loose or sloppy with an occasional value for **F** (like who doesn't?) as the next **x** came rolling in, but I swear: if the measuring tool was as good as centimeters, then that old spring would do just as the good hooke says and do her wanderings and deviations way down in the millimeters where they belonged. No fanfare no big spreads. no worries. And who suffered for that? That's right – no one – and no one back then was prattling on about perfection either. Not if the marking lined up, no, no need to look no further: perfection? Hunting perfection with rods and clocks, rod, spare us all, is like looking to keep

your family warm through winter with the latest in iambic pentameters. . .
mercy… mumble…"

So. The other end of the spring was attached to a rigid wall. The whole situation was oriented horizontally. Just another spring day. But then somehow, you know, things got a little stretched, and, well, ….

Witness Huque account continues:

We measured a displacement:

The mass was sitting **4 cm to the right** of its equilibrium position.

We measured how hard **the spring was pulling to the left**:

our instruments said that the spring was pulling **to the left with 15 Newtons** of force. We then put the mass in a new location and measured again – got a new measurement for force. For each new position, we tried and measured, we'd get a new number for force. We tried a total of 7 distinct positions and obtained the following measurements for force exerted by the spring (to hold the mass in place).

Displacement (cm)	Force (N)
4	15
6	17
7	24
10	32
15	46
21	68
33	102

8.   from b to a

(c) at approx. 32 knots

ooking at the data, does Witness Huque's

account, on the whole, seem essentially CREDIBLE* or essentially NOT CREDIBLE**?

OK: Here's a little more of a definition for each side of the question so that you can feel as confident as possible answering. This definition will then stay right and relevant for a good long while.

* (An essentially) 'CREDIBLE' report a report which we do not see a problem receiving and using as plausibly accurate, that is: a description of events which does not in any significant respect seem to contradict our current understanding of physics law: a report of something that seems like it could have happened – whether or not we actually have active evidence to suggest that particular witness actually observed that particular thing.

** (An essentially) 'NOT CREDIBLE' report a description which seems somehow inconsistent or contradictory with statements we had been otherwise holding as true. (A NOT CREDIBLE report could, moreover, contain its own complete set of statements which contradict one another – but that's atypical.)   In the dominant case, the threatened or contradicted outside knowledge often consists of statements we are holding as true without any conscious recognition or scrutiny until an inconsistency of this sort arises. If/when we come across descriptions which cannot be true at the same time as some other set of claims on which we have relied, then some degree of mental traffic jam is assured until one of the two sides gives some way. We will tend to deem the witness report NOT CREDIBLE – at least at first. If both sides continue in conflict, it's possible our sense of the truth might eventually swing in the other direction.

SO… Back to the question… Those numbers for the spring force/displacement trials. CREDIBLE? NOT CREDIBLE?   It is entirely your choice. You can choose either one. Really, And live to tell the tale. Catch? No—how could there be a catch? What's to catch? Your choice – 'credible' or 'not credible' and that's it. No sweat: A little support, maybe some learning, contemplation of matters like lunch, lose your cell phone charger, wander from the topic and then straight back to phone (damn-still

76

no charger). What could be the catch?

Oh yes: that one. Right – one thing about all these things. Forever in physics and always for sure in Infinity Court and eternally all places else: Don't believe the hype: You have a choice, sure – between p and not-p (between Coke and Pepsi or Democrat and Republican or cancer and diabetes or, here, credible and not credible), but yes: There really is no choice about it. You cannot opt out. Not: You may not. You certainly may if you can, but you cannot and you most certainly may not can. YOU MUST CHOOSE. MUST. CHOOSE. Don't ask: What are the consequences if I don't choose? No—you were never offered that question as a choice. Not even as a hint.

When, with some portion of due respect tendered as a down payment right now and the rest to follow retroactively, do you believe you had you earned the luxury to ask a question – right in the middle of one that was being asked of you, namely to choose? If by some slim chance, you were in the running to be offered last food for thought, well, then, with all the remaining due respect, it would seem you've forfeited by just presuming to ask a question just that like that, no? No warning, no transition, just expecting a couple of pitiable punctuation marks to carry the weight of the word because you don't want to make a simple choice? Well, It's now entirely out of the question. Not choosing does not lead to consequences; consequences have already led to you musting to choose. And only partly, we might add, because the choice is utterly simple and of making the 'wrong' choice here, there are practically no consequences whatsoever. What? Ah. Well, fine then, of course. Quite right. Another simple misunderstanding. Good good, let's all do: Choice coming – one and all.

v.   Final instruction here and we are ready to commit to our choice (report credible? report not credible?):

If you find the report largely CREDIBLE (more reasonably believable than not), then show why you're willing to accept it:

If the story seems to hold up, that is, then it seems to fit somehow with other stuff you know or believe. Connect a few dots, so to speak; add the next detail or two that you could somehow know to be true even though you weren't there. OK, we'll try to be clear and consistent ourselves:

If you believe the report is on the whole CREDIBLE, then, in this case, for example, you could/would:

Determine a value for **k** that would work here.

Use that value for **k** to predict a next ordered pair of measurements.

If you find the report largely NOT CREDIBLE, then in some ways, your job becomes, for a moment, slightly more straightforward.

Presumably, you find it not credible because some part of it contradicts something somewhere – it's at logical odds with maybe another part of the same account or maybe some claim somewhere else. Simply point out the contradiction!

Or perhaps something in the report is inconsistent with simple empirical facts as you understand them – rather than with words. That is, there are ultimately two overarching authorities governing all laws beneath: The Law of the Excluded Middle (for deductions) and The Principle of Induction (for managing empirical data – evidence from the senses). Is it perhaps from the latter source that you take issue? Do tell!

The courtroom has been cleared. Fresh start. New day. An

entirely new witness walks in. This one is some kind of artist. Beret. Goatee. Black clothing, white pancake makeup, a hoop earring and an unexpected tendency to snap his fingers almost desperately while trying to talk but being somehow drowned in volume by the utter absence of any sound that so uninterestingly permeates the docile room, you cannot even call it tense or awkard or 'too quiet' or anything cutely paradoxical that might explain why snappy the jazz witness is eeking out the West Side Story overture rather than taking the floor long since his – when gradually: an enormous poster-board is wheeled out to an easel and all turn to gaze.

The witness contorts into a caricature of someone who wasn't at all expecting to receive the Oscar and is therefore caught off guard wrapped in nothing but rhinestone underwear and the notes for a 20-minute mimed performance of acceptance speeches throughout civilized history. The poster is a graph, to wit:

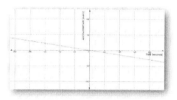

Presumably, this witness is claiming his poster as an accurate representation of (the graph he made from the data obtained for) an authentic Hooke's Law-obeying spring.

CREDIBLE? NOT CREDIBLE?   Why/Why not? (Just like above – if credible, what is, for example, K? if not credible, what's the problem? With what?)

The witness mimes something you eventually understand to mean: HE USED A MASS OF 2 Kilograms. Truly he did. Knowing his first graph might cause a stir, he has therefore made and brought a second graph and claimed that it, too, represents real data from a real Hooke's Law obeying spring – possibly the same spring:

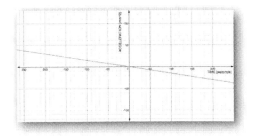

This one: CREDIBLE? Not Credible? Why/why not?

If credible, does it come from the same data as the first graph? How? How not?   If not credible, what changes would have to be made so that it credibly related somehow to the first graph?

Note: For such seemingly rigid matters like scientific law, telling the truth and lying, our definitions have a soft quality. This might be a little confusing. We are not defining witness who are definitely correct vs incorrect, nor even telling the truth vs. lying: We might wish to, but how could we possibly know (i.e. **measure**) something like in someone else's head like that? All we can reliably assess is whether a witness seems more or less worth taking seriously – perhaps hearing again on other details (or not). Our basis for that is whether a witness's way of describing is more or less consistent with everything we have heard to that point.

The central delicate point here is a kind that will come up again and again:

The line dividing between two choices might not be perfectly sharp. There might seem to be some overlap, fuzziness or other sources of uncertainty spilling one option into the other. All true and quite common. NONETHELESS, you MUST still make a choice – and whichever choice you make will then unfold into its consequences as though everything were the perfect black/white dichotomy that we all just agreed it not to be.

So:

Identifying contradictions is often satisfying because – in a way – you know once you've done it. But you do have to be careful: When you select and present a statement which seems contradicted by the testimony, you must have reason to be confident that the statement is well-known and accepted. That is, it must be from physics.

Generally, the only statements we are safe to assume or use are ones that have been explicitly established already. When we are first setting out (now), we do not have a very large number: we have a very small amount of knowledge until we start accumulating some.

This season, we intend ultimately to consider, critique and somehow collect ten statements on the road to our final ruling. That might sound like a very small amount of knowledge for this serious a season of study,

But for statements of real substantive content, which we try and try

not from all different angles, and for which our commitment will actually make a practical difference in somebody's life, ten is probably way too many.

Until we arrive at ten, the only statements on which we are explicitly allowed to rely at any point are:

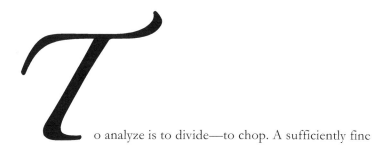

9. *of reference to frame*

The Speed of Stasis

To analyze is to divide—to chop. A sufficiently fine

analysis of the nature of physics leads eventually to grains of astronomical density. *Relativity* is this preternatural dust from which physics comes and to which it ought perpetually to return. It is part of why we cared to look up and listen four centuries ago: The *Terra* is not necessarily *Firma* (Galilei, 1610, p. 63). It is part of why we care to tune in now: Even *The New York Times* has reported subatomic particles traveling to the past (Overbye, 2011). Regarding motion through nature and the nature of motion, physics educators often find themselves caught in some form of the tension described below; the tension contributes to a prevailing sense that prior misconceptions impede the pursuit of effective epistemologies, but the source of the tension can slip away from precise identification—if even consciously noticed. The tension is this:

Having constructed solar system models from grocery produce since they were in third grade, a great many American high school physics students can appear comfortable to the point of boredom with the notion that their floor slips—continually and super-supersonically, no less. Somehow, an ungrounded ground seems to have been internalized as a starting assumption, rather than as a mind- shattering derivation. A good joke, it turns out, loses much in the telling if it begins with the punch- line. This joke is on physics teachers: We may have thought that the moral of the archetypal Galileo tale involved the triumph of scientific skepticism over dogma, but, ironically, Galileo's finding has become the new divine right.

Permeating countless strong and central arguments in classical mechanics is an understanding that emerged with the advent of possibility that the Earth might be moving without our sensing it.

The understanding is that uniform motion, unlike acceleration, is not a thing to be sensed at all. The perspective, experience and measurements of two uniformly moving observers are all equivalent— even if the magnitude and direction of the two motions are distinct. Neither the Earth nor any sun is characterized by inherent velocity or by an inherently preferred status on the stage of space and time. Since Einstein (1905, p. 1), we refer to such equivalence as *Galileo's principle of relativity*.

Flipping the Curricular Vector

As a central premise underlying the doing of classical and modern physics, it has come to function as an assumption behind the teaching of physics. On face, such correspondence—between the raw discipline and the 'PCK' (Pedagogical Content Knowledge) of physics—might seem natural or at least reasonable. In this context, however, the treatment of Galileo's principle (GPR) as an implicit postulate is inverted and de-motivational when contrasted with the alternative: building curricula so that the relative nature of motion is presented as a bold and explicit conclusion.

Recognition that motion is a relation and not a property is fundamental to the practice and *nature of science* as navigated by physicists. It is fundamental to the kinds of conceptual change we struggle to effect and observe in students. Misconceptions surrounding tacit beliefs in absolute or ethereal velocities (and thereby "inertial forces" and "Normal accelerations", etc.), are continually studied and confronted in contemporary modeling curricula. A partial solution sits in the theoretical lens through which this study will be conducted. The solution is not necessarily easy to execute, but it is simple: Build physics curricula toward and around, rather than from, the relativity of motion.

Import of the Principle

In the context of this paper and proposed study, the *Principle of Relativity* refers to the following statement and a number of its corollaries, two of which are found below:

The Principle: The laws of physics hold in all inertial reference frames.

Corollary 1: No experiment can be performed to detect an absolute velocity through space.

Corollary 2: 'Velocity' is a relation, not a property.

Galileo's recognition represents both how we solve terrestrial problems and why we find them celestially significant. First, assimilation of the principle is central to a command of the comparatively concrete standard curriculum: classical mechanics. Vector addition, Newton's first law of motion and Newton's third law of motion are all natural extensions of the symmetry captured by the principle (Newton, 1687, Scholium IV). Conservation of energy, conservation of linear momentum and conservation of angular momentum can all be understood as consequences of the homogeneity of space, the homogeneity of time and the isotropy of space (Noether, 1918, p. 206).

Again, the customary topics crystallize to fundamental symmetries initially suggested and/or demanded by the principle.

Second, the relativity principle is central to an appreciation of the comparatively abstract curriculum: modern mechanics. Einstein's *special theory of relativity*, a crown-jewel requiring mathematical tools no more advanced than trigonometry in order to navigate, rests on two postulates.

Einstein's introduction of the first is dramatic: "We will raise this conjecture (the purport of which will hereafter be called the 'Principle of Relativity') to the status of a postulate" (Einstein, 1905, p. 1).

Third and finally, recognition of distinct yet equally valid perspectives plays a role in maturing past a cognitive-developmental stage of egocentricity (Piaget and Inhelder, 1958). The term 'relativity' has been appropriated and applied to countless discussions regarding ethics, aesthetics, culture and politics (see, for example, Harman, 1975; Quine, 1969). The power of metaphoric or analogical reasoning, however, relies on firm comprehension of the seemingly familiar thing to which the unfamiliar is being likened (Gentner, 1983, p. 158). If any extra-physical implications are to be drawn from the scientific reality of relativity, then misunderstandings regarding the physical meaning ought to be minimized.

Insufficient Treatment in Contemporary Curricula

Relativity tends to be emphasized to a comparatively small extent in contemporary curricula. The canonical undergraduate text devotes no more than two explicit sample problems to the principle. Its green-boxed conclusion stresses the invariance of acceleration but not the relational nature of velocity (Haliday, Walker & Resnick, 2010, pp. 73 – 75)*. The Galilean principle itself is not stated, much less discussed, until the retrospective context of Einstein. For whatever reasons (to be considered preliminarily below and pursued by this study), both the Galilean and Einsteinian consequences of the relativity principle are grasped weakly by statistically significant numbers of contemporary students (O'Brien Pride, 1997; Matthews, 2005).

In standard introductory physics courses relativity is treated with directness and depth only after the conquest of sufficient prerequisite material. In above-mentioned text, it is chapter 37 (Halliday, Walker & Resnick, 2010, p. xiii). The principle of relativity lies, however, at the foundation of the usual topics. Authentic mastery is simply not possible without it. The principle makes no reference to quantity. Impediments to student comprehension cannot be reducible to struggles with numerical computation nor symbolic manipulation. The study described and proposed in this abstract seeks to determine the extent to which improved comprehension of the relativity principle can be fostered by improved techniques in verbal presentation, visual presentation or both.

DOCKET 203

10. of results to lament

Aboard Earth's surface, amidst any given cycle

ofWilcoxon Results. If non-normalized distribution is acknowledged and *Wilcoxon Signed Rank Test* is deemed appropriate, then the comparison between pre- and post- FCI tesdeployed in place of a *t-test*. Unlike the Exam Problem findings, however, we here found statistically significant results which indicated some kind of positive development (*Table 2B:*

Wilcoxon on FCI). The core group consisted of 18 students all of whom were present on both testing days and all of whom completed all 20 questions on each test. From the test taken pre-curriculum (iteration '*alpha*') to the test taken post-curriculum (iteration '*beta*'), the mean score rose from a 7.5 to 13.4 (out of 20).

ts shows high statistical significance, *p* < *.0003*.

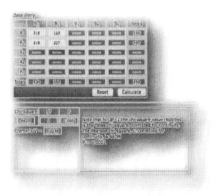

Train of Thought. 5CQ for SAMPLE. by question, not participant. Chi-Square: p < .0001.

ANOVA tests. ANOVA was applied to the data from *ToT*, but the results did not show statistical significance (see Appendix VII).

Train of Thought.

5CQ for ALL POPULATION.

Chi-Square: $p = .027$.

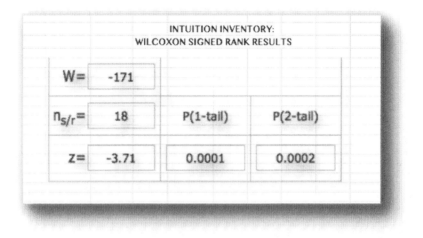

INTUITION INVENTORY: WILCOXON SIGNED RANK RESULTS			
W=	-171		
$n_{s/r}$=	18	P(1-tail)	P(2-tail)
Z=	-3.71	0.0001	0.0002

Intuition Inventory. Wilcoxon Signed Rank: $p < .0003$ from Wilcoxon Signed Rank.

Train of Thought

Chi-square tests. Each of the following five questions contains the essential phrase '*Is* _____ *moving?*': Q1, 6, 11, 16, 21. They are therefore identified as *The 5 Central Questions* (*5CQ*).

Of the total roster of students who started the course, 88 submitted complete responses to both the pre- and post- *Trains of Thought*. From here on, the 88 students are referred to as the *Population*. Of the full population, 18 submitted responses to all components of the study. They are from here forward referred to as the *Sample*.

When the 5CQ responses from the full *population* were organized by participant and analyzed, the Chi-Square Test showed statistical significance, $p = .027.$

When the 5CQ responses from the *Sample* were organized by question and analyzed,

the Chi-Square test showed high statistical significance, $p < .0001$:

FCI Scores: September vs December; Statistic: Wilcoxon SR

Then, In 2013 - 2014, students at different stages of and past the 203-204 physics sequence were invited back and to take a second look, this time while being watched: Results from this eye-tracking perspective were surprisingly illuminating. And follow:

A Study in Visual Cognition Regarding Galileo's Principle of Relativity: That the Laws of Physics are the Same in All Uniform Reference Frames.

Kelly Song, John Jay College
Daniel A. Martins Yovernbaum, John Jay College

Abstract

Introduction

Methods

Results

Results cont'd

Conclusions

References

Acknowledgements

11. from ω to a

Any/all Definitions of any relevant term

whatsoever, particularly when we remind and gather everybody by providing definitions right out in front, no matter how obvious they might seem. The definitions most useful in this context are from physics. The basic definitions at hand are:

1) A **position** is a point in space.

2) An **instant** is a point in time.

3) **Space** is the interval between two events which is measured with a ruler (divided into **meters**, in this system).

The **displacement** between two points is the size of the spatial interval along with some means of indicating direction – using one +/- to distinguish a degree of freedom for every additional axis of space. Quantities like displacement that include a measurement for direction along with magnitude are known for our purposes as vector quantities: Vector quantities allow for otherwise meaningless negative values and thus:

The vector quantity **displacement** can be defined most efficiently as:

the difference between final position and initial position.

4) **Time** is the interval between two events which is measured with a clock (here divided into **seconds**).

5) An **event** is a point in spacetime – like the ordered pair referring to one dot or datum in a customary scatter plot.

6) **Average velocity** means total displacement per total time, i.e. total change in position per total time elapsed.

7) **Average acceleration** means total change in instantaneous velocity per total time elapsed.

8) **Instantaneous velocity** means the average velocity between two points in time – but for an interval which of time which is 'arbitrarily' small,

i.e. smaller than the smallest possible interval detectable by your finest measuring equipment. Instantaneous velocity, that is, is a measurement of the average velocity between two moments so preposterously close together that the velocity could hardly have fluctuated any measurable amount from the "mid-value" So, instantaneous velocity refers to the measurement that is as close as you could ever need or request for how fast you were going literally right then and there – right AT the one point in time the cop pointed the laser at you – or whatever the distinguishing one mark might be.

In summary, an instantaneous quantity refers to a measurement made at or for a single value of some variable. Such quantities are extremely useful for analysis (computations, inferences, etc.) we do in our heads, but they are hard to arrive at.

An average quantity, in contrast, is a measurement made for an interval or region found between two values. Things can change between a region of any finite size, so whenever we wish to assign a single number to a whole interval like that, there is no one single perfectly right one. We do the next best thing and pick the one number that is as wrong in one direction as it is in the other. This is called the average value. Average values for regions are not quite as powerful as instantaneous values for points, but they are much easier to compute and conceive.

9) The **work** (measured in Joules) done on a mass traveling between two points in space is the Force exerted on that mass (in Newtons) multiplied by the displacement between the points (In meters). Work is the scalar product of two vector quantities: The scalar product is computed by multiplying the length of one vector (say, for example, the force) and

multiplying it by part of the other vector (say, the displacement). In this example, we would multiply the length of the force vector by the length of the displacement component parallel to the entire force vector. We are thereby multiplying the extent to which the two vectors share an axis – the extent to which they are mathematically interacting with each other. The answer we obtain, a measurement of Joules of work, is the scalar product of two vectors. It does not have direction, but it can be positive or negative, depending on whether the force and displacement point in essentially the same or essentially opposite directions.

10) Galileo's **Principle of Relativity** (any form).

11) Newton's Laws of Motion (1,2,3).

12) Newton's **Law of Universal Gravitation.**

13) Any basic definition or relation among geometric and trigonometric functions, the group of which we distill and crystallize with a particularly relevant and illuminating version of the Pythagorean Theorem:

14) The approximately constant rate of acceleration at which things fall near the surface of Earth is given here as g ^{2}.

15) The Work/Energy Theorem: The net positive work done on an object, measured in Joules, is s the amount of kinetic energy, measured in Joules, gained by that object. What Work IS (definition): influencing another object (or system) so as to effect change in that other object. The most elementary case perhaps is pushing something to a new position. What Work DOES (theorem): transfer the capacity to do so. When you

change the (for example) position of another object, you increase its ability to pass on that influence to some other – and you have transferred this incremental ability precisely at your own expense. Work transfers energy; energy is the ability to do work. Kinetic energy, specifically, is the ability to do work by virtue of motion.

16) Recently established: Surrounding the 15 bits of knowledge above, we have but a little more with which to work:

We have whatever knowledge we get – once we get it. So, each of the ten numbered equations becomes fair game to use in subsequent analyses   once we've past the corresponding date and established the truth or falsity of that claim.

Today, for example, is Day 1: We are attempting to establish or deny the truth of $F = - kx$. We cannot use it to do so – that would be circular reasoning, i.e. not reasoning. But once we figure out a way and get through Day 1, then $F = - kx$ is part of what we know.

In subsequent matters, we should understand that we are allowed to make use of $F = -kx$. But more than that, we should understand that we are encouraged to do so. We went to it first on purpose; it is hardly a coincidence that we thought about it when we did. So it is a hint for an upcoming matter, as will be that matter for….

17) Long since established: Finally and primordially, we have all the power and all the constraint accorded us by the two most foundational foundations of all:

a) **Aristotle's Universal Law of the Excluded Middle**: For any proposition, **p,** it is necessarily the case that: **(p v ‒p)** or, equivalently, **‒(p & -p)**]. We will sometimes refer to this as the principle of noncontradiction or even just 'logic'; indeed, it is the presupposition on which all syllogisms, deductions and analytical inferences rest.

b) **The principle of induction**: Patterns of observation/measurement that have sufficiently accumulated in the past tend to persist into the future. It is this principle which empowers us to refer to our tables, measurements, sensory stimuli; that is, to our **data.**

ARTICLE II. DOC KET 204

12. witness: in re a hue or two

(a) at approx. 5 knots

t the end of a fine but long day, Yellow and

Pink remained. Yellow leaned against a tree stump. Just then, as you may
recall, a man who needed a haircut "came shambling along, humming a

tune." He carried off the two. This much we know. We do not know where they were taken or what was said or who the man was. It seems that we are free to speculate. For all we know, the following matter is what was discussed. For all we know, what wasn't discussed is what was really the matter . . .

Shambling Man: I would like to show you both something.

Pink: How exciting!

Shambling Man: Well, you ought not get too excited. It is really nothing.

Yellow: Come, come. Nothing is nothing. Something to show us is definitely something. And something is anything but nothing. That is, no nothing is something. And no something is nothing. So show us what you will.

We are excited no matter what.

Shambling Man: But that's just it. I wish to show you nothing. I have heard of one empty box in the empty closet of an empty room in some empty house off No Such Street. Inside the empty box is half a hole. Within the half hole lies nothing. There nothing lies; this is the truth.

Pink: I know of No Such Street. No place looks quite like it. But how can an empty closet hold an empty box?

Shambling Man: Well, a full closet can fit no more--no room for socks, no space for a box. If an empty box is to fit in some closet, an empty closet would seem the best bet.

Pink: But a closet containing a box cannot be considered empty.

Yellow: Yet a box of nothing can hardly be considered full. A closet full of a box full of nothing is a closet full of nothing. And if you ask me, a closet full of nothing is an empty closet.

Shambling Man: I do not wish to ask you anything. I wish to show you something: that is to say, nothing. Will you not join me north to No Such Street?

Pink: I have no interest in nothing. If you have nothing to show us, then I have no time neither.

Shambling Man: Could I interest you in a life of pure joy?

Pink: Of course.

Yellow: Who would not wish for a life of pure joy?

Pink: Nobody.

Yellow: OK, maybe nobody, but what does nobody know?

Pink: Nothing.

Shambling Man: My point precisely. What could be more appealing than a life of pure joy?

Pink: Nothing.

Shambling Man: So, then, nothing is extremely appealing.

Yellow: At the moment, indeed, I find nothing appealing. I also find nothing clear.

Shambling Man: We think alike. I find nothing perfectly clear.

Hence, I repeat my request to visit No Such Street.

Yellow: Well, I would certainly prefer not to sit and stare at these walls.

Pink: Right. We are in the mood for excitement. A fruitless journey is certainly better than nothing.

Shambling Man: Do not forget: Nothing is better than a life of pure joy.

Pink: But from those two points, it seems that a fruitless journey is better than a life of pure joy.

Yellow: Somehow, that cannot be right.

Shambling Man: Yet somehow, it cannot be wrong. Please, I beg of you. Let's stop bickering about nothing. Let us go see some of it instead.

Pink: Perhaps. Perhaps we will join you. Perhaps we will travel to No Such Street. Perhaps we will visit the empty house with the empty room with the empty closet with the empty box with the hole with half missing. Perhaps we will examine the remaining half hole and perhaps we'll find nothing.

   Then again, perhaps we will not. One never knows where one never goes.

Yellow: Say we do. Say we travel to No Such Street. Say we peek in the half hole in the empty box in the empty closet in the empty room in the empty house. Say we peek and find nothing there. What then shall we do?

Shambling Man: Glad you asked. Once we've found nothing, the fun's just begun. Once we've found nothing, we wrap it quite tight. We wrap it in darkness and we steal off in the night.

Pink: If we must, we'll protect nothing with everything we've got. But for what purpose? What point? To what end will we keep nothing?

Shambling Man: To watch what happens next.

Yellow: What could happen next? What could happen to nothing?

I've never seen something happen to nothing.

Shambling Man: Nor I as yet. Legend nonetheless states that in some cracks between moments, for some reasons no one can grasp, nothing becomes something. You might say "no way," you might even say "bull," but occasionally empty just turns into full.

Pink: Now we've gone too far. There's no turning back. Nothing comes from nothing. That's an obvious fact.

Yellow: Pink's right. Something cannot come from nothing. All big somethings come from small somethings. Small somethings come from somethings smaller still. Even a speck of a smidgen must sprout from a seed.

And a smidgen speck seed must be tiny indeed.

Shambling Man: Nothing comes from nothing. That certainly seems impossible to dispute. To make something, then, it would further seem that we must start with something.

Pink: But if we need to start with something in order to make something, that's not really making something. That's already having something and watching it continue to be something.

Yellow: Well, perhaps one kind of something can sometimes become another kind of something.

Pink: I am sure that it can. But say we really want to make a fresh something, no matter what kind. If we start with something, we have not really made something. We've only changed it from one kind to another.

Yellow: So it appears that if we wish to make something, we must in fact begin with nothing.

Shambling Man: Nobody could have put it better. Now can we please go visit nothing and watch it become something?

Yellow: Fine, we're game. Nothing appeals more. But by what dark arts will nothing become something? If nothing is nothing, whence comes the first move?

Shambling Man: From what spark comes the fire? Fair question, my friends. The answer is deceptively simple. To turn nothing into something, all you need is a Kree-8.

Pink: I once heard of a Kree-7, but what, pray tell, is a Kree-8?

Shambling Man: The Kree-8 is miraculous thing. Some say it was invented long ago by someone named Anselm of Canterbury. Others say it was discovered. Either way, the Kree-8 can turn nothing into something. The first 6 Kree models could only turn stomachs. The 7th could turn heads, but the Kree-8 could turn nothing into something. It does not get much better than that.

Yellow: All right, then tell us all about this Kree-8. What does it look like? Where is it found? How does it work? What fuel does it burn? From what was it made? Were two Kree-4's required to produce a Kree-8? . .

ARTICLE III.DOC

KET

382

13. from Ox: to enter & incorporate

(a) at approx. 93 knots

*P*roceedings *of the Infinity Court*

For the 3rd Loop, Axis 18

Session Beginning February 2017

The Hon. Ox the Effervescent, Presiding

Docket 382, S17

- <u>*Executive Summary in re: Pre-Trial Motions*</u> -

1.   *Now before this court,*

to enter and incorporate into the record for Docket 102.S17, being the session beginning February 2017 and ending May 2017, and having assigned without exception all available session hours to the hearing and settling of the matter named below, a single action of no small weight nor passing concern to this court, let this here now be notice from certified diary that distributed at regular intervals throughout the above described session to come,

There come <u>Ten Motions</u>.

The court will hear separately these ten motions and so render separately its opinions. It prepares, as in the normal course, to call on representation for the petitioners and on the characteristically wide array of witnesses, lay and expert, to which this court humbly declares debt for its great and unmatched repute. This court also prepares to invite, in deliberate and emphasized exercise of its faculty to do so, briefs from any and all 'friends' of the court (amicus), owing to the highly particular and grave nature, admitted above, of a sole matter which finally joins into a single trajectory then ten otherwise distinct motions to come before us.

2.   *Ever the way of this Court:*   As long as a motion be one of

which the court finds favor, then any relation or declaration found therein shall be by writ adopted and absorbed into executive annals; all terms of the motion to avail henceforth as reference, guidance and/or compulsion in the settling of future questions involving matters of similar or related concern. A motion here so granted thus becomes, unless and until it be reversed by equivalent proceedings, a wholly assimilated element of the body and history of this court's rulings – bearing no less weight and no more scrutiny than any other like element. All such elements together comprise the sole source of precedent and common law appertaining to the settling of future matters within the jurisdiction and endowed with the full authority of any such element, once having been so integrated for any duration whatever.

What we find for (e.g.:) Motion #3 is therefore expressly

subject to consultation and application

in any question regarding (e.g.:) Motion #4;

in no manner whatsoever, however,

may we refer to Motion #4

when engaged in consideration of Motion #3.

3.   *All Ten Motions are brought before this Court,*

in the order brought, so as to perform associated and cumulative functions – the full collection of which together constitute, this court is given by counsel to understand, one large and intricate argument being advanced by the defendant – in the one large and intricate matter now, and for all the remaining session, before this court.

The encompassing matter to which   Docket 382 of the *Infinity Court* for the 3rd Loop   now and for the remaining session dedicates its full attention is the swift and equitable settling of the question raised by counsel for the plaintiffs in:

"Entropy vs Isotropy",

aka

"The Case of Effect and Cause"

in which

a gang of hoodlum 'virtual' (unlicensed) particles were driving recklessly through some abandoned translucent media on the other side of the Thompson tracks and

were flagged down by Officer i.j. Manifold of the 13th geodesic.

Officer Manifold identified himself but received no cooperation. The gang allegedly continued to move at horrific speeds but reversed course — effecting a state of confusion that will have begun to plague Manifold as many as months before this most unfortunate event.

Directly prior to entering the police academy, therefore, Office Manifold did the right thing and issued a summons to the entire ensemble (having difficulty distinguishing any one particle from another):

for traveling at unlawful speeds
in the wrong direction down a one-way time vector.

The particle gang was arraigned ⸺
4 months prior to all the above.
It has been read its tensor transformations
and comes here before us.
Officer Manifold would, of course, be here too,
but he is now an adolescent, a legal minor,

114

and not entitled to serve as witness.

Attend we now; Presently, we shall ask:

Particle Ensemble, known unto yourselves

as the *Tacheon Gang*,

you have been charged with:

One count of traveling the wrong way down Time Avenue

(at the intersection of Axis X)

&

One count of traveling the wrong way down Causality Way

(at the intersection of Axis Z)

How do you plead?

In light of the matter's gravity,

This court feels duty-bound to remind all who observe:

This court has been, as was averred above,

broadly recognized for its

singularly thorough,

scientifically objective and ethically enlightened

administrating of justice.

By such acknowledgment, this court is only further humbled

And prepared to undertake its present duties,

In service of its role

As 3rd –to-highest in the chain of appeals

For the jurisprudential structure serving loop 3, Axis 18

of all
United F.R. Traffic Courts.

Electron bless the United F of R
Submitted this day,

The Hon: Ox the Effervescent,
Loop 3, Axis 18

15. from Ox to clocks

respecting precedent				faithfully serving time
$\lvert \sin^2\theta + \cos^2\theta = 1 \rvert$				$\vec{v}_{ab} + \vec{v}_{bc} = \vec{v}_{ac}$
				$\sum \vec{F} = m\vec{a}$
Witness:				$\left(\sum \vec{F} \cdot \Delta \vec{x} \approx \Delta \left(\frac{1}{2} m v^2 \right) \right)$
Feb. 1	*Moons, Io, Callisto, Ganymede, Europa (& Roemer*	1.		Light Moves: $v < \infty$
Feb. 8	*A Ripple Tank of Water; A Diffraction Grating*	2.		Light Propagates: $\dfrac{\partial^2 y}{\partial t^2} = v^2 \dfrac{\partial^2 y}{\partial x^2}$
Feb. 22	*A Telescope; A Particular Star*	3.		The Earth does NOT DRAG the Ether: $v_{Ether} \neq 0$

March 1	*An Interferometer;* *Mr. Michelson,* *Mr. Morley*		**4.**	The Earth does NOT *NOT-DRAG* the Ether: $\sim \left(V_{Ether} \neq 0 \right)$
March 8	*Mr. Maxwell*		**5.**	The Ether Permeates All-Space: $\dfrac{\partial^2 y}{\partial t^2} = \dfrac{1}{\mu_0 \varepsilon_0} \dfrac{\partial^2 y}{\partial x^2}$
March 15	*Mr. Einstein*		**6.**	Postulate #2 (is True): $c_{ab} = c_{ac} = c$
March 22	*The Earth*		**7.**	Postulate #1 (is True): $V_{ab} \neq V_{ac}$
March 29	*Mr. Pythagoras;* *A Light Clock;* *Some Muons*		**8.**	Time Dilates $\Delta t' = \dfrac{\Delta t}{\sqrt{1 - \dfrac{v^2}{c^2}}}$
April 5	*A Magnetic Field*		**9.**	Space Contracts $\Delta x' = \Delta x \sqrt{1 - \dfrac{v^2}{c^2}}$
April 19	*A Capacitor; Mr. Pythagoras*		**10.**	Causality Constrains $I^2 = \left(c \Delta t' \right)^2 - \left(\Delta x' \right)^2$

16. of flaws to consider

Summary of Finding from Qq3: Verbal Expressions

The findings regarding pictures and problem-solving in part contributed to a particularly close look at the language domain. To summarize a large number of facets and details discussed through much of the remainder of this paper, the findings regarding *verbal expression* (in general, language) seemed to indicate that the importance of reference frames and importance of the relativity principle had gotten assimilated somewhere along the way by students, but either insufficiently or improperly.

From the verbal responses to *ToT* and *RFR* (analysis presented above) and from a number of the interviews, it seemed that when a very explicit question about a reference frame was asked, a correct answer could often be expected by a good percentage of students. But, in the absence of direct instruction, *when* such knowledge should be applied or *how* it should be applied – that seemed to be lost in translation. Even toward the end of a full semester, the *explicit problem-solving results*, among other areas, indicated: There are times when relativity would be useful and yet it is not invoked, and, conversely, there are occasions on which awareness of relativity is inserted unnecessarily. The notion of relativity might have seemed (to the instructor, at the outset) too simple to allow for such confusion, but such was not the case.

Observations and Conjectures

Choice and Obligation

From the start the principal is presented as a freedom: whereas you (the student) might think that the laws apply only in one context, it turns out they apply in many – in fact an infinitude. So it seems that you can choose the context in which you set out to apply the law, if you are a student solving a physics problem. Here, *'context'* refers to reference frame or velocity.

The problem is that, the selection of reference frame is, in fact, not a choice. The laws of physics apply in all inertial reference frames, but they do *not* apply in *no* inertial reference frame. That is, some reference frame is necessarily in place once the laws are applied. The reference frame might not be consciously selected by the physicist or student solving the problem, but it is selected nonetheless. It is selected implicitly the moment the first measurement is chosen and inserted as a value for some variable in some equation. Whatever reference frame was assumed by that measurement is assumed as a choice. If another measurement made in another reference frame is inserted as a value of a variable, a contradiction ensues and a wrong answer follows, but it is plausible and quite likely for this particular reason for inaccurate results to pass unnoticed.

In other words, the choice of reference frame, when it comes to solving problems, is not actually a choice; it is an obligation. No matter how seemingly obvious, the proper solving of any physics problem ought to start with a conscious designation of reference frame and proceed with a conscious and ongoing check that all measurements have been made in that one designated reference frame.

Comparisons and Contrasts: Relativity as Opposed to What?

Velocity vs. acceleration. Primarily from student responses to the Likert-scale questions posed at the end of RFR problem as well as from responses to the interviews, a distinct concern was inferred: The excitement, exhilaration and seeming liberation of (this curricular emphasis on) relativity can be transmitted to students; it can contribute to increased enjoyment for physics (a motivation for the instructor's choice of this curriculum, as per Chapter 2, and presumably conducive to student motivation). The concept, however, seems to risk being almost too much fun or too liberating. That is, the precise scope and proper use of the concept, particularly when not to use it, might not be so easy to transmit.

It is extremely tempting and common to present the relativity principle or the relativistic way of thinking as an improvement compared to the old way of thinking, that is from Aristotle's. But this is not good enough. Relativity, at least the kind at issue here, currently operates in contrast with other ways of thinking that also do and often should live operationally in the present. If relativity were the only way to think – even in physics – we would not have to struggle so continually and assiduously to emphasize it. The crucial role of the relativity principle, rather, is this: The quantities which are governed by it are indeed governed by it fully, rigorously and in ways that make pragmatic differences (viz. quantitative predictions, solutions to problems, etc.). But such relativistic quantities (most particularly, *velocity*) are noteworthy for precisely that reason; they are not all quantities.

The point is: ***GPR*** explicitly and significantly applies (in classical mechanics)

122

to *velocities*, not to *accelerations*.

The relativity principle, that is, highlights and/or posits a crucial piece of the meaning of velocity and does so by implicit contrast with that of acceleration.

Inertial reference frames vs. non-inertial reference frames. This is very subtle. It is extremely problematic even on the teacher side. The question is: is the principle of relativity a statement about what is true with in inertial reference frames or is it the definition of an inertial reference frame? That is, when we tried to conceive of the physical consequences that might unfold in an inertial reference frame to which the laws of physics do not apply are we picturing Aristotle's physics or are we misunderstanding the term inertial reference frame? The distinction is sufficiently subtle to prevent full discussion here. The relevant consequence of the distinction, however, is that some reference frames are perspectives and are coordinate systems and are worthy of consideration for a physics class, but precisely as examples of reference frames which we should consciously reject when setting out to solve a physics problem. There are indeed reference frames which are wrong to use and wrong to choose but even more wrong to ignore for fear of accidentally choosing without even knowing it.

The central example involves a block on an accelerating incline plane. The question is asked: "at what rate must the inclined plane accelerate horizontally the block remain stationary relative to the plane? "

This is a very simple problem to solve as long as we stay in the lab reference frame but that is a very not simple choice to make -- or at least it is not the common one.

The pragmatic concern at hand is: when we tried to teach and appreciation for inertial reference frames, we mean as opposed to what? First and foremost, we mean as opposed to NO reference frame, but our findings suggest some success in that area. Second, we mean as opposed to an accelerated reference frame, and that is where success seemed less pronounced. One goal of an introductory physics class is to provide good explanations for familiar phenomena such as water remaining in a circularly swinging bucket or the moon remaining in orbit around the earth. Such familiar phenomena often engender equally familiar but incorrect explanations involving terms such as "centrifugal force". At this stage of physics, we have the means and perhaps duty to explain without the use of such misnomer's. Similarly, we might feel a duty to set things up so that in advanced mechanics courses proper explanations for concepts such as the centrifugal and Coriolis effects can be studied and comprehended.

Bearings **vs. comparatives;** *bearings* **vs. interactions.** A significant problem in demanding that students comprehend the relational character of velocity is that *relation* is such an expansive and elusive category. The fundamental point is that velocity is a two-place predicate, space but there are many such predicates of kinds against which we mean to contrast velocity, but rarely address in any direct way.

Let's look at 'bigger than' as a common colloquial version of the scientifically important 'more massive than'. It is certainly a two-place predicate, but it is NOT the kind we wish to teach here. In fact, it is an extremely misleading two-place predicate for two reasons: first, it represents a huge class of similar to place predicates — likely so much huger than the class containing velocity that students would tend unconsciously to picture it when told to picture a to place predicate; second, 'bigger than' is simply a variation on 'big' — a predicate of which we can easily conceive in one place form. 'Big', in other words, is a meaningful way to describe one object. But velocity, according to physics, is not. In order for students properly and truly to conceive of velocity as a physics concept, we demand that they UN-conceive

of any and all other uses of the word. That it is not sufficient to start applying velocity comparatively — that they already do — we are asking them to stop applying it any other way and accept our insistence that the other applications are not incidentally unwise, but analytically incoherent. This is very tough because such other uses are not incoherent when extraordinarily similar words are substituted for 'fast', such as 'big'.

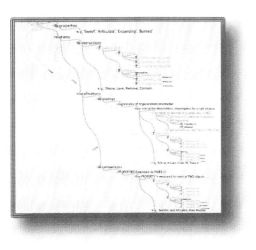

Velocity is a relation, but it is not, in sum, the kind of relation to which we will here refer as a 'comparison' (see figure). It is also not, however, an interaction. At some point in – and then during a great portion of – standard physics classes, forces are taught. And emphasized. Intensely. Newton's 2nd and 3rd Laws, along with 'free-body-diagrams' and usually two to three fully dedicated chapters, all collaborate to drill in the essential meaning of force as interaction between two material objects.

This denotation of force is literally without exception, whether the interaction occurs in a fundamental form 'at-a-distance' (without physical contact) as in gravitation or in a compound tactile form (as per approximation) such as friction. To say that a force acts is to say that one distinct object pushes or pulls another.

'*Exerts a force*' and/or '*experiences a force*' then, is quite necessarily and significantly two-place in physics. To *force* is to commit an action accurately describable only by means of a transitive verb: If a subject but no object can be identified, something somewhere is wrong in the physics. (The **field** concept differs in precisely this respect.)

So, force as interaction is a very large and very central part of the basic physics curriculum. Unfortunately, it again represents a type of to place predicate which we do not wish to use when constructing a model for velocity — except by means of explicit contrast.

When a first object has velocity relative to a second object, the first object does not interact with the second object. By this we mean the following: imagine a third object observing the first two. If the first object were removed, the third object could expect to observe a change in the second only in the case where the first had been described as exerting a force on the second, but not in the case where the first had been described as having some velocity relative to the second. Put more simply, the velocity of A relative to B does not affect B (in any customary sense of the word 'affect'), but the force from A on B does affect B.

Velocity is thus neither a comparison nor an interaction. To the extent that it is a relation, it is a highly unusual one. It functions more in the manner of a preposition. In this study, we come to call the type of relation velocity seems to represent a 'bearing' (see figure).

We are saying, therefore, that an essential feature of 'velocity' is its requirement for 2 objects, but we are also saying that two highly familiar sets of predicate forms which share this feature ... share it in the wrong way. Worse, the two categories to which it would be wrong to turn for analogy or comfort or comparison are categories that play vital roles in physics –

roles we DO wish to emphasize in other contexts. The second one, interaction, is particularly insidious and crucial because (net) force produces acceleration. And acceleration is NOT velocity. The distinction between velocity and acceleration is of top conceptual priority to any physics teacher – whether the teacher is focused on kinematics and calculus (1st derivative vs 2nd), the units of scientific measurement (m/s vs m/s^2), the basic operation of Newton's Laws (1st vs 2nd) or, as here, the scope of GPR (applicable to the former, not to the latter).

Worse yet, all the above represents thoughts and inferences discovered as a result of analyzing the findings from this study. As to the extent to which these linguistic observations account for or correlate with — much less 'cause' – inadequacies in a typical mental model for velocity we dare not speculate. As to the importance of these observations, however, we insist. It seems fairly hard to dispute that they are true — that is, that velocity is a relation which is neither a mere comparison nor an interaction — regardless of what terms we choose in making this observation. It seems very hard, however, to argue that they are obvious or at the forefront of consciousness whenever any of us is teaching physics. They certainly were not known or noticed by this instructor until after the fact of data collection (and twenty tears of teaching), i.e.: arguably "too late".

Reference frames vs. positions. In stressing the importance of a reference frame, we do mean to stress the importance of a perspective. By perspective, however, we mean a characteristic of the observer which necessarily affects the observation. This concept might not be new to students; they might well have encountered it in some branch of visual arts. The challenging wrinkle in our physics use of the term perspective is this: the determining characteristic (of observer which affects observation) is not location, but rather motion.

By reference frame, then, we most explicitly do not mean vantage point. We mean something larger than a point --something like a frame. We mean a coordinate system. We mean a choice of origin and choice of axes, perhaps 2, perhaps 3, perhaps even more, but in any case necessarily axes that are mutually perpendicular and individually identifiable by no special characteristic other than that (angular) relationship among the group. This coordinate system then necessarily sits nowhere, but travels continuously from somewhere to somewhere else at a rate which is to itself necessarily nothing, but somehow something — of great importance — to something else.

Without some kind of mental model for this traveling grid, physics is not a scientific investigation of space and time, it is an abstracted set of computational exercises (what some students might consider 'math'). And a mental model is necessarily visual. But this visual necessarily involves change in time, so any visual depiction requested of students must be sufficiently sophisticated to capture or convey such change.

The coordinate system, furthermore, is not a concrete real thing about which we construct mental representations, nor is it even a representation. It is a representation of a means through which or by virtue of which we construct representations, so any mental model of a coordinate system must be singularly abstract and sophisticated to say the least.

Vectors vs. vector addition. A means of graphically representing the appropriate mental model is provided by vectors. Of course, vectors are not known at the beginning of a physics class. Eventually, vectors might help a student offer the kind of drawing we might like to see, but this assumes a successful learning of vectors. The problem in two-dimensional velocity addition, meant to be conceptually central, might have been distractingly weighted down by just this assumption: that vectors were understood by students.

The world of vectors is a world of mental models unto itself. Eventually, this model succeeded in revealing student conceptions -- but not in the manner intended.

Vector finding one: A reference frame is the zone in which measurements are made; it is not the zone in which analysis is performed. Analysis, that is, is independent of reference frame. Vector finding 2: the seemingly straightforward instruction "to add vectors, place them tip to tail" entails a jump from one reference frame to another — within the same drawing (if we're dealing with velocity vectors). Victor finding 3: placing vectors tail to tail (an operation which is generally not encouraged) keeps vectors in one reference frame. That addition and subtraction should produce such a fundamentally distinct mental pictures is a huge observation that might well be among top instructions when attempting to build a mental model — except that, like the linguistic observation regarding *bearing*, it is utterly NON-obvious – nowhere within the conscious mind of the instructor, at least of this course. How, then, could we expect to find it in anywhere within the mental models maintained or depicted by students?

Legitimacy vs. productivity; justification vs. motivation. We (the physics instructors) insist that legitimate results are discoverable through any of a great number of possible inertial reference frames – an option set, we insist, sure to be larger than expectations. Stop, challenge your first instinctive choice of frame and consider a wider set of possibilities, we say.

Just when a student seems to have started to internalize this advice, just when s/he seems to be considering more than one reference frame in order to solve a problem, however, the student is quite liable to hear us demand "stop" – don't use that reference frame (or coordinate system); use this one. One prominent example involves the inclined plane, where advise a tilted reference frame and struggle to teach the breaking up of a vertical vector into two oblique components. An angled x-axis and a vertical hypotenuse together make an utterly new and counter-intuitive procedure -- except to the rare person who has proceeded through a full solution performed within the customary reference frame, found a correct answer and found that the correct answer required many more steps from the customary approach than by the one recommended in class. Few teachers, it seems, put themselves through this exercise in contrast. It is practically never imposed on students (and certainly does not appear in the standard textbooks, such as Halliday, Resnick, Walker).

This is quite a fine line to draw to a group of people that begin by knowing no physics at all and are expected to cross through the bands to second-guess material that is supposed to be natural organic or intuitive. This is no anomaly in the physics course – at least not in a good physics course taught by somebody who enjoys physics.

This course vs. other courses. The features of a reference frame that we wish to get across and that we wish to be included in a student mental model are also identified, it turns out, by their contrast with features and discoveries that arise in other branches of physics: subsequent courses primarily.

We say that the velocity of an object is meaningful only when measured relative to another object. This is certainly true and important. It is accurate and complete — even in classical physics — as a description of particle motion. Once we transition to wave motion, we need to say something more like "the velocity of a pulse is meaningful and fixed when measured relative to a medium".

When we get to the electromagnetic wave, moreover, we come full circle in a very nontrivial — in fact, historical — way and find ourselves saying that the relation between speed and medium is so crucial that when the medium cannot be pinned down, the relativity of velocity flies out the window and provides us with a speed that claims '*invariance under transformation*': the speed of light.

It is understood that the first class in physics is too early to dive into such matters: all in good time. But what needs to be recognized is that contrast with such dramatic twists plays a huge role in the importance of the pre-twists. That is, our concern for reference frames is in part dictated by hindsight; we are attempting to present foreshadow in the manner that might most effectively allow for final resolution.

To summarize the seven foregoing descriptions of contrast, the concern here is: velocity as a relation is not just an improvement over the way we used to think in physics. It stands in contrast with 1) acceleration, 2) force, 3) position, 4) wave propagation, 5) electromagnetic radiation. It is fundamental to the study of physics not just in the way that it brings the clarity of coherence to such study, but also in the way that it prompts the excitement of paradox and surprise to such study. If only the former (clarity in the moment) is consciously considered while teaching, we risk confusion in future areas which provide part of the motivation for teaching the principle in the first place and we risk confusion in application of the principle itself.

Velocity Vectors

Treatment of *velocity vectors* represented an area in which perhaps the most vivid inadequacies were found to be stagnating within student mental models and, consequently, among the most potentially fruitful sources for a constructive pedagogical response.

Vector Procedures → Drawing Instructions

First, vectors are graphical, visual, representations. Some kind of deployment of something like a vector is what, perhaps, we would like to see in a student's original attempt at visual depiction, i.e.: the first instrument. To be sure, proper vectors are not expected the first the first time we administer any visual instrument: we haven't taught physics tools yet, so we do not expect to see physics tools in use. We might hope to see some glimmer of vectors the final time we administer the visual instrument, but even then it is no requirement. On both occasions, rather, the issue is: do the types of concerns addressed by vectors get addressed in these pictures, and, if so, how? Vectors are not the only way to visually depict magnitudes, directions and changes in either, but they are a highly efficient and familiar way to do so, so it is helpful to bear them in mind as examples when analyzing student data (collected by the visual instruments).

More particularly, there is a list of directions/instructions which becomes implicitly available at the outset of any vector computation. The basic procedure for, for example, adding vectors controls the direction and focus for the problem-solver. This means that vectors add more than a drawing component to a problem-solving endeavor: It adds a strict guide and/or structure for making the drawing. Such structure, presumably, makes the drawing task more approachable both for students comfortable with drawing and for those who are not. The right structure, it seems reasonable to hope, might well raise the chance for yielding informative drawings. Such rules – such specific guidance for drawing – were severely lacking in the 2012 administering of the instruments for collecting visual data. Naturally, that was not the view held by the principal investigator at the time. The sections of Train of Thought which requested drawings did so in what might have appeared to be a fairly specific manner (see figure below).

Once considered in connection with the velocity vector addition problem posed in the *Explicit Problem-Solving Instrument (Qq2b)*, a precise description for the deficiency became apparent (and is discussed below). Though the specific vector findings will shortly be discussed in detail, what follows immediately are excerpts from two iterations of *Train of Thought: Visual Instrument (Qq1a)*. One is the original document used for Physics 203 in Fall 2012. The other was used in Physics 101 in Fall 2016. The pair is presented in order to show an evolution in (at least some component of) the *instructor's* mental model: a growth in what a teacher (this one) pictures when he asks for pictures.

2012

1A) Draw a neat and clear sketch of the situation as you understand it. . .

* * *

[4. The Final Sketches . . .

Draw three final sketches of the situation as you understand it. For each sketch, include arrows to indicate an object's motion. Use larger arrows to indicate greater speeds. If something does not appear to be moving, do not attach an arrow

Figure 2: ToT Drawing Directions, 2012

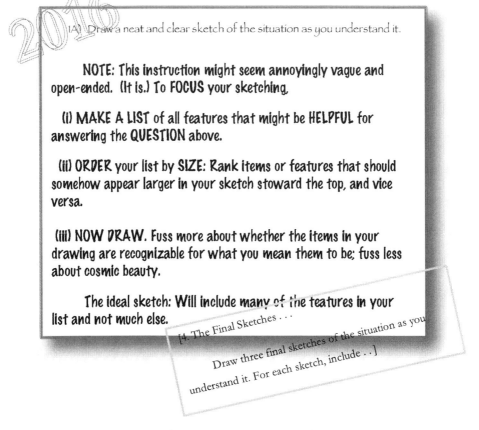

(A) Draw a neat and clear sketch of the situation as you understand it.

NOTE: This instruction might seem annoyingly vague and open-ended. (It is.) To FOCUS your sketching,

(i) MAKE A LIST of all features that might be HELPFUL for answering the QUESTION above.

(ii) ORDER your list by SIZE: Rank items or features that should somehow appear larger in your sketch stoward the top, and vice versa.

(iii) NOW DRAW. Fuss more about whether the items in your drawing are recognizable for what you mean them to be; fuss less about cosmic beauty.

The ideal sketch: Will include many of the features in your list and not much else.

[4. The Final Sketches · · ·

Draw three final sketches of the situation as you understand it. For each sketch, include . .]

Figure 3: ToT Drawing Directions, 2016

Modeling Models → Horse-Trading Abstractions

Second, the world of vectors is a mental model or set of mental models in its own right. The rules of vector construction decomposition and addition comprise a very clean and powerful example of the kind of features with which we identify mental models in general. Vectors embrace a challenging dual character reminiscent of reference frames reminiscent of reference frames: they take something abstract like three-dimensional instantaneous measurements like arrows drawn on the page; they then ask students students, somewhat strangely, to get used to moving such arrows around the page, to connecting them, predicting, and internalizing and trusting their geometric 'behavior' as though the arrows were comfortable, sensate objects unto themselves. That is, vector methods for computation are a wonderful means for imbuing computational outlines with spatial or observable (hence more mentally accessible) girth, but their effectiveness does rely, somehow, on user acceptance of an "arrow"; to get correct answers by means of vectors, one has to transform numbers into arrow properties (length and orientation), write, direct and produce a mental movie about some particular interaction among such arrow properties, watch the end of the movie and then transform the ending back into a conclusion about numbers. This at least one noteworthy round-trip journey through abstract thinking.

Vector Addition → Reference Frame Transformation

Third, the addition of velocity vectors is central in application of the relativity principle (see section regarding *GPR 4*, above). As noted earlier, GPR 4 is fundamental. And once it's operating in more than one dimension (to wit: the '*explicit problem*'), it's all about vectors – specifically, instantaneous velocity vectors and the addition thereof.

An instantaneous velocity **vector**, like all vectors, is an arrow. That is, it is a one-dimensional but asymmetric segment of space. One edge of the segment is distinguished from the other by means of an appended corner or 'tip'. The edge without such supplement is called the 'tail'. The length of the segment (measured in some stipulated set of units) represents the size of some **vector quantity** (some real measurement characterized by a set of special properties) and the orientation of the arrow's tip represents the direction of the vector quantity. If the sum of two vector quantities is sought, the vectors themselves – the drawings – can be used as reliable computation tools. The two vectors must be drawn contiguously, such that the tip of (either) one is in direct contact with the tail of the other. If the two vectors are placed in this manner, then they suggest a unique triangle – one which becomes explicit once a third vector is drawn.

There are two conceivable ways to complete the triangle and draw this vector. If we choose to start it with a tail to join the pair's unmatched tail and proceed to a tip to match the pair's tip, then the length and orientation of this third vector are the magnitude and direction of the sought vector quantity. That is, (one of) the (two) arrow(s) that is essentially forced into appearance by a particular arrangement of two others is 'the answer' to an addition problem we believe the two to represent. All the foregoing is true of vector addition in general. In order to perform a computation, we neither tabulate digits nor press buttons; we move arrows around a page.

The arrow *movement* is the central and insidious agent of abstract action: **Because the one apparent property of vector that does _not_ convey information is its position on the page, the one informative choice we can and must make is: where to place the arrow on the page!**

All the above describes a tricky feature of the mental model we ask students to accept – when using vectors to perform 'simple' addition, an operation which is otherwise not so simple once we allow for more than one dimension.

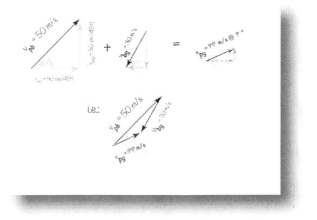

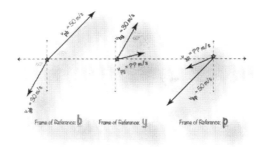

http://www.yaverbaum.org/meTer/GPR4.mov

139

ARTICLE IV. POST TO SCRIPT

17. *from y to i*

ToT Sketches: Inadequately Executed

The sources for visual data consisted primarily of the *ToT* sketches, the *RFR* answers and, to a lesser extent, the response solutions to explicit problem-solving. Generally, *ToT* was distributed during one of the very first lecture meetings of the semester. Students were asked to read, consider and form preliminary responses. They were asked to do so in real-time, as a 'do-now' and 'cold' or 'out of nowhere'. A traditional sense of orientation was, typically, lacking more than would ever recur from that day on.

Distribution of *ToT*, in light of the above, wildly diverges from the norm for a typical semester's *Day One*. Quite a bit, it seems. To ask for work at all is unexpected. To ask for work that does not review work from the past is even less so. To ask for work in science and then say there is no right answer more still. To see that such seemingly open-ended work can be simultaneously so simple and so difficult is also unexpected. To look around and see highly intense debate emerge among strangers – in reference to something of no apparent relevance whatsoever very much so. For whatever reasons, the devotion of *Day One* to the vivacious discourse unfailingly produced by *ToT* is, semester after semester, exceedingly popular among students. If there is one day on which physics morale is reliably peaked, it is right before *Day Two*. Yet the drawings that were elicited via such a seemingly exciting activity were, it had to be admitted, extremely disappointing.

Student verbal answers to the *RFR* questions which were posed in relation to visualizations seemed to indicate fairly specific mental mechanisms and methods, if not strict models. It seemed somehow incongruous yet inescapable that the students, a number of whom could clearly draw, simply did not, via their drawings, have very much to say. Student ways of understanding were not always strong, but they were identifiable; the students seemed capable, that is, of expressing the visual contents of their minds. It seemed they could use words their mental pictures, but they could not make pictures to communicate their pictures. This trend seemed plausible — not self-inconsistent – but nonetheless surprising.

By the winter of 2012, creative endeavors to draw statistically significant or qualitatively suggestive data from the *Train of Thought* sketches felt decreasingly clever and increasingly contrived – sometimes inauthentic. Each new attempt to identify a trend or tendency – to say nothing of a connection or correlation – felt inexplicably strained. Eventually, an un-confirmable but powerful realization surfaced in the form of a conjecture: The surprising and distressing extent to which the sketches failed to indicate was, perhaps, attributable in part to their failure to inspire. Whence this? The sketches, bluntly and judgmentally and unscientifically put, were themselves woefully uninspired. When considered from the perspective of a principal investigator or general research scientist, it was not entirely clear what the description 'uninspired' might be intended to mean. Considered from the perspective of an instructor with over twenty years of experience, however, the biting art review's denotation was as apparent as its accuracy was assured. With near-total trust and without

142

apology, the experienced teacher may well make swift decisions and enact bold behaviors on the basis, plausibly, of hundreds of emotional or social-dynamical signals per day – each of which the instructor will receive in the manner of a self-evident fact and then feed into a response machine with a full bypass run around scrutiny or critique.

Spikes in a student's enthusiasm – or abject fear – or aggression – leap out and onto teacher consciousness, as easily from a student in confusion as from one in command. Similarly, the work of a student might well convey complete competence – even artistry – while it simultaneously transmits a sense of creeping angst – to a pedagogical/emotional receiver built from hard support and sharp doubts contributing in equally negligible measure.

To the instructor of record and concern here, indeed: It first seemed possible and eventually seemed probable that the engagement engines from which the pile of sketches dribbled had been running on fumes. The drawings had been 'dialed in'.

Of course, said instructor was also principal investigator and according to the coordinate system held by the latter, at least, some solid support for believing the sweeping and spontaneous claim above was, to say the least, required. One cannot simply declare the presence of student ennui and expect the hollow declaration to perform any meaningful function in a scientific study. In the first place, by virtue of what possible *reason* should this assertion regarding student moods be treated with any seriousness. In the second place, so what? What possible research or pedagogical gain, if any, professes to wait at the end of some wanton verification chase?

ToT Sketches: Inadequately Assigned

Presumably, on this particular research road, travel should have stopped right there – right as we found ourselves shouting a seemingly unreasoned pronouncement about some dissatisfying day in the life of some classroom morale tides bearing only an incidental connection to the study matters at hand. But, as things turned out, the research direction did not reverse at that juncture because, we here argue, it should not have. The conjecture was that the ToT sketches lacked inspiration or, to choose perhaps a slightly more pedagogically potent term, that the sketches lacked *motivation*. The thought certainly may have had the potential to somehow help, but only if true. Demonstration of such truth demanded, if not further data, reason. What could be the reason for lack of motivation for an assignment that seemed so quizzically and unfailingly liberating semester after semester – the topic that repeatedly dared to regard the first physics class as physics sales pitch day as it attacked syllabus read-along and won back its rightful place on center stage for the opening ceremonies?!

The drawing assignment's lack of appeal was easily read (once looking) in the eyes of the students who were accustomed to drawing – and accustomed to liking it, even under compulsion or assignment. The reason for the hollow sketches was hollow motivation, we conjectured without motivation. The reason for the hollow motivation was that the assignment was un-motivating; the drawing assignment, in fact, was, if lucky, an empty, vacuous and amateurish assignment. More likely, it was not really a drawing assignment at all. Why or how should we come to suppose that? Because we are a physics instructor, not an art (or like) instructor. And we should be ashamed of our physics teaching self – particularly that part of self who bragged about the twenty years clocked. The twenty years, evidently had been necessary or at least contributive to the level of physics teaching expertise believed to underlie choice after choice after subtle choice made

144

amidst the construction of physics assignments. In the one grand semester surrounding sudden self-identification as artist in residence, had a moment's consideration been directed toward the vast unknown arena of pedagogical content knowledge for art? Had drawing been contemplated even slightly as an independent discipline (as we would certainly and haughtily insist for physics) or were art skills being assumed as anything but and the mountain of thought tending to bolster even the seemingly simplest physics assignments condescendingly assumed to be needed only for real courses – like physics?!

The assignment for sketching was a bad sketching assignment. Consultation with colleagues readily revealed this to be the case. What, specifically, was bad about it? All, specificities, that were missing from it. Asking somebody to draw, leaving it at that and then wondering what was wrong was like asking a group of physics students to find speed. Period. Under utterly unspecified conditions and at or for utterly unspecified cases. We would expect very little from students in response to such assignments. The drawings revealed little because the drawing assignment asked for little. The visual data had, in fact, indicated something of significance. The weak data suggested a flaw or two in the instrument. The flaw in the instrument consisted of a failure to provide a set of specific directions/instructions for guiding the drawing process.

And why had such a list not been created? Because it had not even occurred to the designer of the research – that visualizations were that sort of thing. At this point, the deductive chain was growing excitingly long. Perhaps a bit too long. Or too exciting. There were quite a few inferential steps we seemed to be stating and stepping on – as though incontrovertible. Did not some piece of this elaborate deMorgan's demon need somehow to be proven or argued somewhere? Yes, if any of the steps were actually to carry meaning. In fact, however, what popped off the stack was the very last step – the sole step needed:

Why had it not even occurred to the instructor to write a set of directions? Because such a set would direct our thinking somewhere – from not visualizing at all to visualizing something specific. Presumably, the journey to the visualizing of something specific should be easy to break down – if the something specific to which the journey sojourned was known. I had imagined nothing at the end of the road, so no set of sub-partitions revealed themselves to me.

Entering the ToT zone, that is, I, the instructor, was in possession of *no mental model* for no thing. The first development demanded was of the instructor mental model – from nothing to something.

The above realization was at once mortifying and motivating. Above all, however, it was self-evidently true and almost as assuredly as important. It had been prompted by a series of claims, each of which was indeed highly subject to doubt. But so what? The steps did not need to be proven at all because they were not going to be used. By means of psychological association rather than of analytical implication they had led to the true finding and, like the dummy variables of mathematics, they were now quite welcome to take their toys and go home. Having been sufficient to suggest the real finding, they needed not be necessary. And what, again, was that real finding? That a person could teach physics for twenty years, spend a number of the latter years musing deeply upon mental models, design and immerse in a research study meant to crack the physics pedagogical code by taking a deep long and critical (condescending?) look at student mental models, and somehow never once even consider the need to take a look for his own.

It was strange enough to notice that I had never bothered to ask myself for mine. A little spooky to consider the possibility that hesitation was prompted by intimidation: It suddenly seemed like quite a hard assignment. It was near paralyzing each time I caught myself starting to create the elements of the model I would claim as mine. If I had truly been doing all this physics for all these years without one, then what was the meaning of all this research?

So, what was my model? It certainly had to fulfill the four criteria adapted from Etkina, Matilsky & Lawrence (2003) and discussed at the outset of this paper. The observations presented directly above, however, seemed to point to additional requirements for a mental model designed specifically for the laws of motion and specifically for this curricular context. I either had to retro-fit or self-discover architecture in my mind that somehow integrated all of the elements below into a dynamic, visual and simple yet potent representational tool. Really, toolbox. This cogitation garage to be the instructor mental model must, it seemed, satisfy the following descriptions:

a. It must principally feature some kind of image of a coordinate system or vista – not just a picture of a thing as viewed from a particular perspective, but a picture which emphasized perspective itself as an agent.

b. The visual depiction of this coordinate system must be sufficiently vivid to stress allegiance to a particular side for each of quite a few dichotomies: inertial not accelerated, referential not interactive, for measurement not for computation, etc.

c. Though specific as per above, the right model must work for a broad swath of varied instances, lest it be a thing not a model. All models must predict. The physics instructor's model, moreover, must especially point up this very versatility of application as at the heart of the course material. That is, the reference frame recommended for today's problem-solving context is justified by the gains it winds up offering to tomorrow's. The mental model must contain both.

d. As we would expect of any coordinate system, this model would probably have an origin, but it should not be overly tethered to it: This coordinate system is somewhat akin to a zone, but it refuses to be, finally, a region. The typical mental model arises precisely to battle the misconception of a perspective determined by position. If the instructor mental model for reference frames did not explicitly distinguish itself from a place, then whose would?

e. The distinction between a position and a reference frame (or velocity) is the passage of time. Any system or phenomenon worth modeling, presumably, is characterized by some sort of time element. And any mental model for a reality of any sort, moreover, demands by definition a time element. But here the thing to be modeled was not just a dynamic thing. It was a thing for which data showed disregard for the time element to be a significant misconception.

A mental model for the laws of motion would seem, in other words, to carry an elevated duty to communicate time. A mental snapshot is not enough. A picture is not a model. There seemed no way around it. What seemed to be the distracting inconveniences and confusions riddling RFR due to a highly amateurish animation were not tangential and were not incidental. I needed animations made and I needed to learn how to make animations – sufficiently, perhaps, to then teach how to do so. This became a very large undertaking. And it consumed a great deal of instructor time from 2012 to 2016. Consider the following...

Perhaps, then, consider the following.

2012 Instructor →

http://bit.ly/rfr_2012

A century ago, perhaps, no one could make an animation so no one expected it in a physics classroom. My colleague counterparts of the 1800's were off the hook, but not just for lack of competition. No one was watching animations, so no one held prototypes or models for that form of expression. Five years ago, many teachers and students conversed fluently in the mode of the moving 2-D image standing in for 3. Just not me. If I speak poor Spanish in front of two-year-old, I either entertain or annoy him with the melodies of pure drivel. But if I speak poor Spanish to a native, I come close enough to a real form of expression that my errors can be taken just seriously enough to cause authentic misunderstandings or frustrations. In 2017, in other words, mental models for physics principles like that of relativity had better involve some solid animations.

2016 Instructor →

http://bit.ly/newton_shell_theorem

An effective animation is a little movie (and one that often distills certain elements such as dimensionality or color). A movie tells a story.

The familiar mesmeric rhythms of a physics curriculum, as discussed above, waltzes from rising action and mounting expectations as we approach the problem to be solved, the direct engagement with conflict and paradox as we seek to solve, to what is often a strangely satisfying surprise in resolution, and a denouement to direct us back again. *The oldest good cartoons were good shows – even though they were not* (even by tolerant cinematographer standards). Therefore,

    f.   The mental model must be more than dynamic. In order to grip and hold and play with memory without abusing it, it must be in some manner convey ***narrative***.

2016 Students →

http://bit.ly/gamov_creek

    g.   It must not only allow for trial and error, but for discourse and dialogue. For right, wrong and reasoning and rejection. It must embrace ***argumentation***.

    h.   Grounds for choosing one frame over another often came from the future – findings to which the students in question could not possibly have been exposed. Sneak peaks at closing chapters can help motivate through the tough chapter. But they can also function as spoilers. When introduced subtly and helpfully, a nod or two toward future is a foreshadow. Even or exclusively when it appears before or during the present. We have hidden answers in the titles of exam problem; we have placed them on files outside faculty offices. The advance answers do help and students love to believe that they are clever explorers of hidden treasure as they cover their tracks and get high scores. The easiest way to corrupt our chances for the improved outcome, of course, is to remove the secrecy and label the whole as a *'PROOF*.

i. If each is to be my mental model or yours or hers, then every last one of them must accomplish all the above, yet no two should be identical. A mental model is supposed to help make a translation within and by means of a particular mental landscape. It must add or subtract an extra flavor that somehow makes reference to the context in which that mind is uniquely situated. My mental model, ultimately, is no such thing unless it is *personal*.

2016 Students →

http://bit.ly/crazy_jjtrain

http://bit.ly/gpr4_mm

The model must be personal. It must actually be for and by its keeper.

For four months, he directed explicit and demanding attention toward the mental models held by his students, continually insisting to know about their features and their growth. During no time did he offer up even a reference to his own. Does this demonstrate an exceedingly selfless and empathetic spirit to his communication? Is he listening so hard that he neglects to speak? Or is it the reverse? Is he so snobbishly caught up in his own role that he cannot be bothered with the slightest moment of obvious connection and just give a try to the directions on which he insists?

He claims to have trained all concerns and probes tightly on the minds of his students: He would like nothing more, presumably, to glimpse what is going on their minds. But no physics background whatsoever would be needed by any but the most heartless cold teachers to recognize the basic way in which students are stuck from even feeling accountable to take any step at all until somebody shows them, matter-of-fact, first example.

If the instructor begins to create and present a mental model of his own (a model for modeling), it begins to verge on somewhat elaborate – at least more than that of the typical student's. Even given feedback or another model to juxtapose, it runs a risk of hogging focus in a class discussion. It is about the instructor not the students. So which really was the 'right answer'?

Are *you* in the model? Where? How often?

In one of the earliest steps taken toward the analysis of qualitative visual data, every *ToT* sketch was coded with at least one – often more than one -- positive integer ranging from 1 to 10. Originally, we expected to be able to group the drawings into a scheme which more or less resembled a 5-point Likert Scale (though without any particular size ratios among the different groups), but the generally simple drawings did not lend themselves to mutually exclusive categories. Instead, therefore, the codes below were used. They seemed like great overkill, but were deployed in the attempt to assign codes to all conceivable descriptions – rather than straining in circles to build codes around drawings and then find such codes to be of substantially less use at the next collection of drawings. Given sketching instructions of the form 'Draw x from the reference frame of y' and 'Draw x from the reference frame of z', every sketch could be coded with at least one of the following marks.

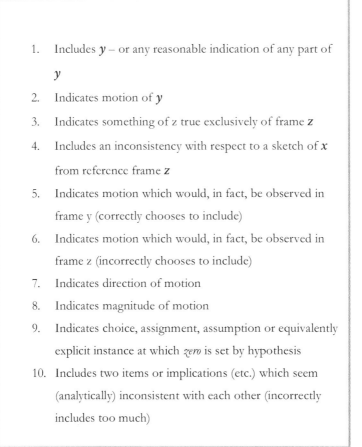

1. Includes y – or any reasonable indication of any part of y

2. Indicates motion of y

3. Indicates something of z true exclusively of frame z

4. Includes an inconsistency with respect to a sketch of x from reference frame z

5. Indicates motion which would, in fact, be observed in frame y (correctly chooses to include)

6. Indicates motion which would, in fact, be observed in frame z (incorrectly chooses to include)

7. Indicates direction of motion

8. Indicates magnitude of motion

9. Indicates choice, assignment, assumption or equivalently explicit instance at which *zero* is set by hypothesis

10. Includes two items or implications (etc.) which seem (analytically) inconsistent with each other (incorrectly includes too much)

The first two were examples of the attempt (described directly above) at completeness: Though as early as possible in the physics semester, it hardly seemed worth the ink to prepare codes for drawings to include explicitly the reference frame from which the drawings were supposed to have been observed – much less to indicate motion for such frames. Yet a great many such inclusions were found: It was not uncommon to see a prominent figure of a subway car, for example, within the sketch assigned to show what was observed from that subway car. Such inclusion represented about as large a departure from the meaning of reference frame as could be conceived – more of one than anything consciously expected – but not one that ultimately served to show a statistically significant evolution of mental models. Why not?

In the first place, the prominent appearance of a reference (and thereby inappropriate) object in sketches was not generally so wrong as to be accompanied by indications of motion (such as arrows). Indications of motion tended not to be managed very clearly or creatively with respect to any part of the sketches. There was not much specificity to infer or say about the reference frame, therefore, other than its role was fundamentally misunderstood. In the second place, the presence of y in pictures meant to be drawn from the reference frame y recurred in the second round of drawings – to approximately the same level of frequency: just frequently enough to be disappointing (to show no evolution in this respect) but just infrequently enough not to constitute (it seemed) a statistically significant finding. This flaw seemed to sit steadily and unremarkably enough not to warrant real analysis, largely because of the factors described above: It seemed just small enough not to evolve, yet it certainly indicated a misconception demanding corrections. To a lesser but real extent, a similar presence -- of observers within data meant exclusively to depict the observed – was noticed in verbal responses to, for example, RFR and interview questions. The sporadic misplacement of reference frames presented a buzzing irritant to an instructor hoping to optimize comprehension, but, to a researcher investigating evolution, presented no particular course of analytical action. Upon confronting what appeared to be a glaring need for an instructor's mental model, however, the small but steady student tendency to step into his/her own field of cognitive vision seemed slightly poignant.

Where in a useful *instructor* mental model (a role model for models, so to speak) prompted this messy but noticeable aspect of the ToT drawings, might we find the instructor? Here, the working definition for ***frame of reference*** (a distinctly abstract sort of construct, even once specified in a particular example) seemed to collide quite unhelpfully with the working definition of ***mental model*** (something, once specified, meant to be palpable, visual and, in this context, personally specific). If the instructor's mental model for a reference frame were to somehow include the instructor himself, would that not dangerously transmit or encourage a substantial misunderstanding? If, however, the instructor's model made suggested no presence nor hint of the instructor, then how would the mental model stand out as being personally or particularly associated with the instructor – how could it, that is, *instruct?*

Metaphor

The above might well all be metaphoric, but not accidentally. A fundamental requirement of our models is that capture dynamism and the passage of time. But the principle to be conveyed is precisely that all flows through time are indistinguishable from one another and indistinguishable from no flow. Velocities are depicted by vectors, which very deliberately sit still on the page.

So the particular feature we insist on graphically conveying is the stopped character of time. Necessarily, we are trying to abstract an abstraction or communicate a non-literal feature of a literal phenomenon. So the mental model must be concerned, at some level, with cross-applications and metaphoric meanings of 'perspective'.

I am the instructor. Home base for all my analogies is teaching and curriculum.

What follows, then, is the mental model which has evolved for me in response to the findings and non-findings of which I struggled to make sense over the last 75 pages and the last five years. It embodies, among many other implications of the above, a recognition that the P203 curriculum had been designed with too much awareness of physics curricula implicitly surrounding it – but only implicitly. My current model for understanding velocity, frames of reference and the laws of motion is, for better or for worse, unmistakably a model held by the instructor – and offered to the students over time. It is not a curriculum; it is a programmatic bundling of five curricula: currently underway for three out of the five pieces. In order to incorporate the above discussed demands for imagery, flow in time, narrative, curricular glimpses forward, argumentation, proof, shifts among various perspectives, metaphor, analytical rigor and situational specificity, the following mental model might be better understood as a *classroom reference framework* or perhaps most honestly as simply a classroom role - playing game environment.

It might be called *Infinity Court.*

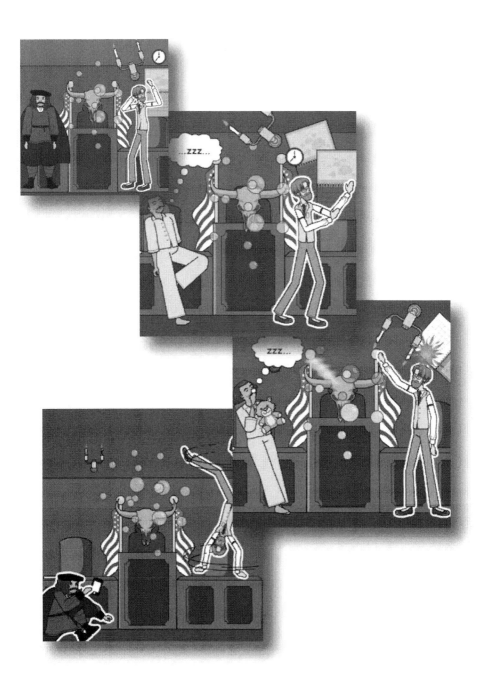